I0049122

Quickbooks

Run Basic Bookkeeping Tasks in Quickbooks

(Techniques for Business and Personal Account Management)

Ashley Smith

Published By **Darby Connor**

Ashley Smith

All Rights Reserved

Quickbooks: Run Basic Bookkeeping Tasks in Quickbooks (Techniques for Business and Personal Account Management)

ISBN 978-1-77485-516-4

No part of this guidebook shall be reproduced in any form without permission in writing from the publisher except in the case of brief quotations embodied in critical articles or reviews.

Legal & Disclaimer

The information contained in this ebook is not designed to replace or take the place of any form of medicine or professional medical advice. The information in this ebook has been provided for educational & entertainment purposes only.

The information contained in this book has been compiled from sources deemed reliable, and it is accurate to the best of the Author's knowledge; however, the Author cannot guarantee its accuracy and validity and cannot be held liable for any errors or omissions. Changes are periodically made to this book. You must consult your doctor or get professional medical advice before using any of the suggested remedies, techniques, or information in this book.

Upon using the information contained in this book, you agree to hold harmless the Author from and against any damages, costs, and expenses, including any legal fees potentially resulting from the application of any of the information provided by this guide. This disclaimer applies to any damages or injury caused by the use and application, whether directly or indirectly, of any advice or information presented, whether for breach of contract, tort, negligence, personal injury, criminal intent, or under any other cause of action.

You agree to accept all risks of using the information presented inside this book. You need to consult a professional medical practitioner in order to ensure you are both able and healthy enough to participate in this program.

Table of Contents

Introduction

In this guide, we're going to provide the most advanced methods tools, techniques, and methods in QuickBooks that let you easily manage and manage all the financial records for your business in the most impressive manner. We will explore various techniques and methods that will not just help aid in making your day to working life easier but also let you create and access all the required data you require.

The first step is to explain the strategy you can employ to safeguard your company's files from loss and corruption before moving on to advanced inventory management and valuation techniques. In addition we will also discuss the different tools can be used to have your company's operations run in just a few seconds. Then, we'll move to the most important part of your business's operation. This requires sophisticated cash flow and cash management managing techniques, using the latest systems for sales and management.

In this article, we will examine the most important methods of managing the cash and making sure that our cash reserves remain protected in accordance with our creditors and our revenue. Then, we'll move to the second part of the cash management and maintenance of cash flow using the purchase system where we will go over the most recent techniques and strategies to cut the cost of payment and keep check on the balances of suppliers.

We will also pay attention different ways to produce advanced reports as well as using advanced reports by using different reports that are combined and self-created reports within QuickBooks. The last chapters of the book will discuss the typical payroll-related issues and problems that can be easily addressed using new and advanced techniques , as well as describing the automated method to have your fixed assets effectively managed.

Chapter 1: Beginning With Quickbooks

Customization

Are you bored of the outdated accounting software and are looking for ways to improve it? Are you seeking ways to import the old files of your company into QuickBooks for you to start working from there? Are you seeking the ability to make QuickBooks to suit your needs?

Many people find it difficult to figure out how to establish their business within QuickBooks when they decide to move from their current accounting software. However, many QuickBooks users would like to make an entirely new company file using the company's old files. But, the possibility of losing important data when transferring company files can be catastrophic.

Perhaps you'd like to setup your business on QuickBooks and not alter any old data. Additionally you might also want to design a design that's for your requirements. QuickBooks is a remarkable digital accounting software that offers many advantages to both you and its users.

So in this chapter we'll cover the following topics that are important:

* Prepare your new company's company file from the old files

The QuickBooks software can be customized to meet your requirements

Should I Restart My Life?

If you're an old QuickBooks user and have found out that your current company data files are beginning to occupy a significant amount of storage space, then your most effective option to prevent these kinds of problems is to make an entirely new company file. It could be because due to the old data being insufficient storage space on your disk or perhaps the files of your company contain corruption bugs or glitches within their structure. In the process of creating a brand new company file, it isn't an easy task which means you'll have to go through the transactions over again. In order to solve this problem, QuickBooks has provided an alternative solution to your problem.

However, before we get started taking a break, take just a moment and think about whether creating a brand new company file could be beneficial. Most of the time it is the case that establishing the company's file isn't enough to solve the problem. For example there is a glitch in the payroll processing which doesn't clear the payrolls which were previously paid. In these cases it is recommended to contact the support department of QuickBooks for a better understanding of the issue.

Another factor to be aware of is whether you are able to establish your new company files following or after the conclusion of the current fiscal year since starting this kind of procedure in mid-year of financial year may result in losing information. The consequences of this decision of yours could have disastrous effects. The best time to begin this task is following or before the end of the year.

Condensing and Archiving your Data

The first thing that comes up is the option of archiving or condensing data. This feature in QuickBooks lets you remove your old data and information unaccessible to you. This is accomplished by completely eliminating your old data from the company's current file. This ensures that no prior data, reports or other transactions, other than the preferences settings and lists are able to be opened in the future.

It is crucial to remember that you should maintain a backup of your whole company's data prior to starting this process to condense your information. This will aid you find any previously deleted information you may require at any point. To get rid of the data and the transactions you must follow these steps:

1. In the menu you'll need to browse to File. Select Utilities and then Condense Data option.

2. Locate the Remove the Transaction option within the condense data window, and then click it.

3. Choose whether you want to erase all information until a particular date or completely erase all data.

4. Afterward, Choose Next -> Begin condense.

After this process has been completed after which you will be provided with additional space QuickBooks can provide you with regards to your company's information files. In reality, QuickBooks only archives and reduces transactions that have been cleared or closed. For example the case where a customer has a balance that is receivable this is an unclosed transaction. When the customer has paid his outstanding debts, it's an open transaction.

Other settings and lists that were created personally by you are not deleted during the entire archiving process.

Migration from another software

It's also possible that you already have an accounting software and want to transfer your information files from QuickBooks. In this case, QuickBooks mostly offers the basic settings that permit users to create a brand new company file and start from scratch. The more advanced setup gives you more precise control to design the interface to suit your needs.

First, you'll need to take the balance of your trial at the end and the general ledger the balance sheet, as well as your profit and loss statements from the previous accounting software. This is that you'll have to prepare the journal entries to start the year for your business. To create the entries you must follow the steps below:

1. Select File> New Company.

2. After that after that, you will be presented with options such as Express Start, Detailed Start as well as other choices. Select the detailed Start.

3. After selecting, QuickBooks will begin the regular procedure in which it will inquire for the Company information, the company's name and other information about your business. Complete all required fields as well as the essential information into the window.

4. When you've completed the information for your company and hit Enter to go to the next window. QuickBooks setup wizard will ask you for information about the customer, details on products or services bank accounts, etc. In the next window.

5. Input all the desired information in the designated fields and rows.

6. When you're completed, click Finish or Start Working near the bottom, and click on it.

QuickBooks will automatically launch the user interface, where you'll have to communicate with the program once you've completed the steps described earlier. The next step is to add all the balances , and then putting the balances in

QuickBooks for the current year. In order to do this:

1. Make sure you have completed the entire checklist of Chart of Accounts, which can be found within List-> Chart of Accounts. Check that your updated chart of account for QuickBooks is exactly like the previous data files for your company. It is possible to align them line-by-line to the names of the accounts in the sample balance.

2. Create an additional account known"Adjusting Equity (or Opening Equity. Opening equity is a good option as a suspense fund to keep the balances that are opening in the ledgers of accounts. It is important to note that QuickBooks automatically sets up opening equity accounts automatically. Opening Equity account when you have entered the balances for opening on your Chart of Accounts edit page for certain accounts.

3. Take through the Journal Entries for all the accounts, excluding the balance of your equity account including trade payables/trade creditor and trade receivables/trade creditors along with fixed assets.

4. Be sure that your net change in journal entry is geared towards Opening Equity, which you may adjust later.

For bank balances as well as other cash items QuickBooks will request the balance of the account at beginning of the set-up process is in progress. For trade receivables as well as trade payables, there are two choices: either you can include all invoices from each trade receivable as well as trade payable through the using the Home screen. You can also include all the information and amount as a journal entry for the entire ledger of accounts without invoices.

In the case of fixed assets there's two options that are available in QuickBooks You can either add all fixed assets that have their written-down value using the Fixed Asset Manager tool, which is available within CompanyManagement Fixed Assets or you can use on the Journal entries. Another method is to include these fixed assets into the Fixed Asset List. The final outcome must be the same since they all have to be able to balance out the adjustment of the Opening Equity account.

After this has been completed after which the adjusting Opening Equity account will have zero values and your balance sheet will show exactly the same figures that were reported by the balance sheet you downloaded from the previous program.

Common Issues during Set Up

It is possible that you will encounter common problems when you are transferring your company's data to QuickBooks. The reason is because you will not be able reconcile your chart of accounts correctly. When you add the balances you may think that the task was done correctly, however due to the advanced system of QuickBooksthat all entries appear balanced, however in the wrong account.

This can be an issue that is not too significant for you because it does not allow you to quickly find any error or missed entry even if the test is balancedparticularly if you're running the business at a greater size or the administration of personal financials can be difficult. Here are a few ideas to be aware of:

* If you believe that you can ensure an easier and more controlled flow of business after switching to QuickBooks you should try to send your Journal Entries in the combined form instead of dividing

the journal entries into separate entries. This can reduce the chance of risk because all entries for a specific account will be combined into one central group.

* Because the new version of QuickBooks offers more sophisticated capabilities, it is advised to enter the balance of the opening during the time that you create Your Table of Accounts in QuickBooks. This will be automatically passed to another entry to opening equity account. Opening Equity account created as the default entry in QuickBooks.

* Accounts receivable as well as accounts payable types don't give you options to input opening balances at the point that you are preparing the Chart of Accounts are being made. This is why it is suggested that the balances for opening of individual accounts be added using both the Customer Center and the Vendor Center for each, and vice versa.

* Ensure that you reconcile all balances after your project. The majority of people not do this and instead start using the program. Reconciliation can be accomplished using the balance sheet or trial balance as well.

Customization of QuickBooks for the individual

QuickBooks comes with the default features that permit QuickBooks to work normally with all users. It doesn't mean QuickBooks blocks you and other users from making modifications to its settings. Its default setting are available within the program to ensure that those who use QuickBooks initially do not end up stuck with a myriad of difficulties or errors.

This feature of QuickBooks gives its users enormous flexibility, which is a reliable software. The settings options are easily customizable in accordance with your specific requirements.

1). QuickBooks Preferences

The preferences are the most basic features that can be observed within your QuickBooks Interface. Preferences that are default, which are in effect after you download QuickBooks include making a tiny noise or sound after the transaction is completed and automatically placing decimal marks into transactions. They also use the most recent dates or the date that was that was entered to allow for future posting of transactions as well as other options.

The preferences window has two tabs, Personal Preferences as well as Company preferences. You can edit them manually on both the tabs. QuickBooks simplifies this process and makes it simple to comprehend and allows users to be acquainted with your specific desire. It is accessible via:

i. By selecting Editand then Preferences in the menu bar at the top.

ii. You can navigate to the tab you want.

iii. Once the changes are made hit enter to save the modifications.

2). Personalized Icon Bars

The icon bar lets us effortlessly access the most commonly used tasks that we complete every day. Icon bars are generally suitable for different kinds of users who are frequently navigating and use the program to make adjustments. This could include the finance or accounts department employees of the company. They frequently make adjustments and modifications to the same company's files in QuickBooks. The icon bar is great when combined with security features, as well as the roles feature provided to these employees.

Icon bar could assist us to navigate through the usual tasks, or assist us to separate the icons according to the roles assigned to every user of the business and the files it holds. The icons that are commonly found on the Icon bar are a majority of the operational tasks carried out by the company including the customer icon which allows us to view all the details of customers' lists, their outstanding balances, outstanding amounts as well as other information.

The Vendor icon lets us collect the information about the vendor as well as create the various job-to vendor reports, and highlight most significant transactions made by the vendor, for example. Other icons, such as Reports, Bank, Payroll Home, and Accountant offer a variety of options for quick access to your various requirements. To alter the icon bar:

I. Click on the View customizing Icon Bar option on the top menu bar.

ii. Choose the desired Icons that you would like to show in the Icon Bar.

iii. Enter or click OK when you're done.

You can also alter the location on Icon Bar. You can also change the position of Icon Bar to display in the upper part or left side, as well as on the left side. This lets you organize the interface better and accomplish your tasks more quickly.

3). Add 3). Adding Custom Fields and Reports

Custom fields permit you to build custom database entries by adding different fields to the data tables. QuickBooks provides an integrated and advanced system that makes sure that your accounting information is entirely centralized to meet your specific requirements for your database.

In the workplace there is a possibility that you will find it difficult to maintain duplicate copies of all client's data. You would not only need to add the list in your specifically developed software, but you'll also need to add the list separately to the accounting program you use. This is the reason why this feature of QuickBooks is particularly beneficial to contractors and service industries.

QuickBooks lets you create an unlimited number of custom fields can be defined according to the type of input data. The input data type is the information you typically enter - whether it be an image, text or in some other form. This will help you create an easier system in which the entire history of a customer or vendor, as well as other employees are available by clicking the button.

This allows you to create custom reports using the fields that you've created. You can add additional fields

I. Go through your Customer Center, Employee Center or navigate into the Vendor Center and click any of these.

ii. Choose an option for creating a brand new employee, customer or vendor.

iii. Click on The Additional Info tab and click Define Fields displayed as a button.

iv. Create the custom fields you want and then press Enter when completed. Press Enter more to save the modifications.

4). Allocating Account Numbers in Chart of Accounts

Experts and advanced users employed a very complex program that uploaded the data from the Chart of Accounts in a sequence of numbers. These were considered to be the sequences of accounts that determined the order in which information was displayed within the General Ledger or the trial balance. It was also used as it allowed the pertinent accounts to be joined into a common account group with respect to.

In QuickBooks this feature is able to be easily used by skilled users who prefer setting their accounts as part the sequences. By default, the accounts' numbers are not visible, and QuickBooks will assign the sequence in secret in accordance with the set sequence in it's own algorithms.

The reason advanced users would prefer accounts with numbers is because it allows them to regulate the clubbing of the group. This can be accomplished by:

I. Moving to Edit> Preferences at the top menu bar.

ii. Choose an Accounting icon in the bar.

iii. Select the Company Preferences tab -> Select account numbers in the displayed accounting window.

iv. Enter to save the modifications and then resume work.

If you are looking to join the accounts by using the sub-account feature, which allows different accounts to be combined under a single category or class.

i. When you are navigating to Lists- -> Chart of Accounts, choose the account you want to establish into an account subordinate to another.

ii. Before you open the sub-account ensure that you've already set up the primary account that the desired sub-account will be classified.

iii. Right-click the account and choose Edit to change the information on the account.

iv. Select the checkbox for Sub-account and then select it.

V. Name of your main account you want to use.

vi. Enter to save the changesonce you're completed.

This will group all accounts into the appropriate major heads. This allows users to quickly create reports and categorize them based on the classes they belong to. These reports will give you thorough analysis of financial data.

Personal finance management is a must This feature could help you in allowing you to separate your primary costs from the extra. From a business standpoint it is possible to categorize the transactions according to locations or regions.

If you run an enterprise of a medium or large size operation, and you need to receive reports that are segregated based on your location and departments, this can be used to classify and segregate every transaction. QuickBooks will automatically generate the report you want immediately.

Pro Tips for Setting up the QuickBooks Interface

It is essential to be informed when you set up the QuickBooks Interface. But, this chapter is targeted at the more advanced techniques to create the user-friendly interface while still adhering to all the essential principles of accounting process itself. Here are some professional tips you need to be aware of:

1. Make sure you define and create roles before setting up QuickBooks in order to protect the integrity of the company's data files.

2. If other users have access to your company's files, be sure you are watching the audit trail and keep track of any changes created by users other than your own. The feature of audit trails is accessible in Reports section, which is under Accountant & Taxes Audit Trail.

3. After you've created the lists and added the other important information into QuickBooksThen, you can secure the lists and the setup to prevent other users from being able to access or modify the lists.

4. Explore the preferences thoroughly to learn about the various settings options available. If you're operating in other currencies , too you can switch on the multi-currency feature to transmit Journal entries into foreign currencies, too.

5. Make sure to turn on the payroll as well as other features. It is crucial to include the employee list prior to turning on the payroll feature. It is possible to access via the internet or manual option (this will be discussed in the next chapter).

6. If you're making a new QuickBooks firm file by using an previously created one, or you are archiving previously created company files, be sure you've saved the backup copies in a different location before creating your company's files for archive. This will allow you to access and restore your previous business files any point.

It's important to remember that you will not have access to the most recent or current company file when you open the prior company files. It is therefore recommended to keep a backup copy the current company file before opening the earlier company files.

Chapter 2: Inventory & Items Management

The management of items and inventory system that is available in QuickBooks is much more advanced and much more efficient than you ever hope for. The system for managing inventory isn't just a simple way to record and keep track of an inventory; can be far more than the standard usage. For the service industries, inventory aren't the only source of revenue. They rely instead on the rendering of various services that are classified as products- there's an item listing which regulates all the items and billing methods.

If we were to define the major sources of revenue by the industry, we'd be in a trading or manufacturing sector that deals with products and services and a service sector that is related to items or services. This chapter we'll concentrate on the most advanced techniques for managing items and inventory which will provide you with the knowledge and expertise about QuickBooks.

1). The latest Inventory Management Methods

managing inventory can be an overwhelming task, particularly when you're handling multiple types of product within your stock. The objective of managing inventory isn't to simply enter the supplier's bills into this system. an efficient and integrated method for inventory management is essential.

There is a good chance that QuickBooks offers a centrally-controlled method to manage your inventory by using various options. These features and management methods are included in the version for enterprise of QuickBooks and you should ensure that you've got it installed.

a). Inventory Management at multiple locations

If you run a small-medium-sized business or perhaps a larger business , it is likely that you'll have multiple inventory locations in different geographical regions. These could be various states, different cities or even countries. In these cases it can be a difficult job to comprehend the quantity of inventory available at different locations as well as the value of the stockthat is in the warehouse.

The only option in this kind of situation is to physically count the inventory and using valuation techniques to determine the appropriate price of stock. This method is employed by the managers of various businesses and companies during the year-ends, or at the time of closing to examine their physical data with the information they have within their system.

The reason we will discuss in this article is that you need to know the price and the quantity of your inventory at any given time. The main reasons you should consider this approach is:

* You will have total control over procurement as well as your inventory distribution system which will permit you to distribute inventory from one central place of operation (head Office) to various branchesand locations.

* This allows you to identify any irregularity that you find in the management of inventory at the branches.

Many branches take orders from their headquarters to prevent fraud. By conducting audits and reports on inventory you'll be able determine whether branches need the inventory or not.

Since the system is linked to nearly all other operational functions The chances of loss or theft of assets are easily averted or monitored.

The first step in making use of Multi-Site Inventory is activating it:

I. Navigate to the desired location and select edit -> preferences> Items and Inventory.

ii. 2. The Items & Inventory window will appear and then you can select the tab Company Preferences.

iii. Within the center of the window you'll see an option for Advanced Inventory Settings. Click this option.

iv. After you have clicked on this option, look for it on the Multiple Inventory Locations tab and ensure that there is a Multiple Inventory Sites checkbox has an X.

It is a matter of. Also, ensure that the shelf, row and bin options are set under the tab.

vi. Enter to save any modifications made, or left-click on OK.

When you turn the feature to multiple locations "on," you will be able to see that on Home>> My Company (located in the upper right)> Inventory Activitiesthe new option called Transfer Inventory will be displayed there. It is also possible to create an additional place for your inventory which could be delivered from your supplier directly to the location or sent that inventory to your customer in your new address.

This is done by simply adding the new location description within the build Assemblies option. Choose the Activities tab on the lower left-hand side of the Build Assemblies window, and then add the new location in"New" "New" choice.

When you're done with this, you'll be able to carry out multiple actions with ease.

* You'll be able to get your inventory directly from the vendor in the location you want. After the bill has been entered and the location is assigned, you can add the location or place to the inventory and instruct your supplier to ship the inventory to the location. It is also possible to designate a new location during the time that the bill is recorded.

Additionally however, you will also be able to sell your inventory to customers who are listed within your list of customer records as the inventory location that you wish to sell from. If you change the location on above on the sales Order you can sell your inventory from the desired location.

* You may transfer the stock from one place to the next through selecting an inventory of the location you wish to transfer, and then selecting the location where the inventory will be transferred. Open the Home window> My Company> Inventory activities transfer inventory to carry out this move effortlessly.

Additionally you can also create diverse reports like the selling of inventory by location quantity of inventory at the moment, inventory valuation according to location, and many other reports that will be created using the location of the inventory.

b). Allocating the Serial Numbers the Inventory

The majority of users categorize inventory items based on the basis of a serial number , or the lot number. Serial numbers are unique and identify an item that is in the inventory. With this method you'll be able to identify and track all items included inside your different inventory areas based on specific serial numbers.

If you own a huge retail store which there are thousands of customers and more than a thousand items in your store, you'll find this feature is extremely fascinating and useful. This feature will offer you an exceptional service when a client discovers a defective product, or wants to assert their warranty or wish to swap it out with a different one.

The most frequent problem proprietors of retail stores encounter is when they request the customers for receipts. In many situations, the customer does not have a receipt. This can make it more difficult to determine if they bought the merchandise from your shop. Fortunately, serial numbers can help you to keep an accurate list of items that are offered for sale.

The first step is activating the feature in QuickBooks. It is important to keep in mind that these advanced features are accessible only in QuickBooks Enterprise. Enterprise Version of QuickBooks with complete access. Follow the steps below:

i. You can go to the Edit menu bar at the right.

ii. Click Edit> Preferences and then Items & Inventory in order to open the Items & Inventory Window.

iii. Choose the tab Company Preferences and then navigate towards the advanced inventory settings.

iv. Locate the Serial Number tab, and then enable to check the Lot and Serial Number option by pressing it.

V. Select the additional checkboxes that you wish to select within the tab.

vi. When you're finished then press enter to save your changes to your company's file.

Other options that are displayed within the tab will comprise various warnings and popups which will be displayed when one of the requirements is satisfied. The criteria you define are yours to decide on, but QuickBooks already provides already defined options to assist your. For example,

* Warning message when your inventory's serial numbers are not filled in.

Warning symbol in the event that the serial number is already being used to identify an item in inventory.

A warning message is displayed in the event the serial number isn't found within the system. This can be helpful in the time of refunds or warranty claims.

After you have completed the required settings There are a number of hidden functions that are not available within QuickBooks that will permit you to include the serial numbers or lot numbers that you would like to add. It is important to remember that serial numbers must be unique and not have a resemblance to a series which has been used previously.

The best method to ensure that you have authentic serial numbers is to creating an excel spreadsheet that contains the complete details of those serial numbers. You can manually create serial numbers, or they could be serial numbers of bar code.

When some retailers purchase products from their suppliers, they usually make use of the same serial number that suppliers have utilized. This method can be beneficial in situations where you don't wish to create serial numbers to track your inventory. However, being a big retailer, you'll find that the majority of suppliers do not use serial numbers. It is therefore advisable to create the serial number yourself as well as lot numbers.

There are many possible uses for this feature as it can streamline your inventory management.

This allows you to trace the total inventory as well as its complete movement. If someone is trying to get the right to a refund or warranty in relation to an item then you'll be able find it within the accounting software.

* You may also trace the item on the base of its serial numbers which allows you to identify the name of your customer and the person who purchased the product.

This feature is extremely helpful in the event that someone needs to come up with a claim to be covered under warranty. Simply look up the serial number within the system and locate the entire process of this particular item. With this method you'll also be able to identify the source from which you purchased the item.

It is possible to access the search feature by clicking the Report section of the menu bar, then selecting Inventory> > Transactions List By Serial Number. Then, you can type in the serial numbers, and the inventory type. This will show all the transactions associated with the serial number.

* You'll also be able to move an inventory item from one place to another location, however this time, it is accomplished by using serial numbers assigned for the inventory.

* You may also go through the Reports section in the menu bar, and then use the latest reports, such as the valuation of stocks by serial number or by location. stock by serial number.

These features are described for serial numbers found in QuickBooks. But, the second feature that is available is called the Lot number. All of the actions and the procedures to use Lot numbers are identical, however this time, in the serial/lot Number tab, you'll need to turn on to check the Lot Number checkbox.

This time , instead of accessing reports via serial numbers, you will be able access the reports using Lot numbers. You can also fill in all your data using Lot numbers you've defined. The purchases and sales are now using Lot numbers. Wholesale businesses in which the products are sold in lots this option is most suitable and adaptable for them.

You should be aware of the kind of business you're operating to be able to control your inventory. In terms of personal management, inventory isn't a factor in your business however, if you are providing certain services, you must go to the items and services section in this chapter.

c). Bar Coding your Inventory

Making and typing the number of serials or lots that you're offering your item to a customer will take up a large amount in time. This is especially the case when the buyer is looking to purchase several items and there are many customers waiting in queue.

Another issue with serial numbers for retail companies and lot numbers used for wholesale businesses is that it could consume the majority of your time entering the numbers into an accounting program. Sometimes, you could add incorrect numbers to the system by mistake and this can cause another item to be added to the list.

Barcoding is a common practice in large retail businesses to prevent these types of accidents. In addition your workers or employees are also subject to a significant amount of stress when they must manually enter the serial number or lot numbers for each item. QuickBooks gives you total control and an automated process using barcodes. This makes the whole process simple to carry out without stress.

Before you can begin using this feature, you'll must first design the barcodes of your products. In other words you can let QuickBooks generate barcodes automatically for your products , making your job easier.

i. Open Files, then Preferences and then Inventory & Inventory.

ii. Then, choose from the Advanced Settings option for inventory.

iii. You can go on the Barcodes tab and click the Enable checkbox for barcodes.

iv. Once enabled, press Enter repeatedly to save any changes in the company's file.

It is possible to use the Barcodes tab also offers the option of using the wizard that allows

QuickBooks the ability to copy or import barcodes that are in a different area and put them in the one you want to. In the event that you do not have barcodes, QuickBooks will assist you with that.

If you would like to add the barcodes for all of the inventory items you want to track in your Excel spreadsheets You can do this:

i. Select Lists> Edit Multiple List Entries.

ii. Select the Inventory option found on the bar of search.

iii. After QuickBooks displays the inventory by list, you are able to add or copy all the bar codes in Excel sheet.

iv. Click Enter or exit from the screen by clicking the Save Changes button to save all changes that were made.

When you're finished making the changes you want to make, QuickBooks will automatically provide you with the necessary features and functions that are connected to barcodes.

It is easy to be able to buy products from your vendors simply by scanning the barcodes of the items using the barcode scanning function of QuickBooks. If you scan an item several times, the amount will increase automatically after every scan on the invoice of the vendor. This allows you to keep track of the inventory without the need to enter code numbers for every item manually.

If you scan an additional object, QuickBooks will add the new item on a different line on the invoice bill to make the process easier and also to calculate the total amount of the invoice.

The same applies when you sell your goods to customers. When the bar code scan the item it automatically generates an invoice that will calculate every item's price at its retail selling cost. You could look up the serial numbers using the same scanner for bar codes.

This is not all it also speeds the process of moving the products or items to various sites of the company. After you've selected the location from which the products will be transferred, look through the items and create the list of the items that are to be transferred to the second site.

With the feature QuickBooks allows you to manage business operations from any place and also keep the entire set up centralized and connected.

You can also modify the various reports , and add the barcode images on the list of prices. This will assist you in re-creating barcodes of items which don't have barcodes or the barcodes of which they aren't easily scanned.

* On top of this, you can make different reports using the barcodes like sales through barcodes, information about inventory by barcodes and so on.

This feature is able to be utilized in conjunction with the various inventory location options and serial/lot numbers feature. When you use all of these features together you'll be able to organize and keep track of your inventory.

All of these features are required for making the management of your inventory easy and straightforward. It is essential that your inventory is well-managed and kept up to date. These tools keep track and balance of each move of inventory.

Important Key Points to Consider on the Management of Inventory

Due to the new and advanced features that QuickBooks has developed it is possible that you will encounter problems when keeping the records of inventory, specifically with regard to inventory management.

* Always conduct the annual or semi-annual count of the inventory that is located in your various locations or at different sites. The count must be performed physically while in the area. This is due to the fact that certain entries may not be reported by the system, which could result in a difference between the actual inventory on in the store and the stock listed in the system.

* You need to do the reconciliation of the entire inventory to find out the exact position of the stock as well as the amount stated on your sheets.

Be aware that a great software for managing inventory isn't the best way to safeguard your inventory. The best practice that firms follow is to provide a full control environment for the protection of their inventory. This means hiring a security guard, installing an identified security device or security camera, for example.

* Also, you must count the cash you have in your register against invoices you have issued, comparing the cash in hand with the cash that is collected from clients. This way, you'll be able to verify that the inventory is sold at their sales prices.

2). Advance Estimation of Inventory and Grouping Techniques

QuickBooks separates the two components of the Inventory system . inventory management and valuation methods. A lot of times the people don't know the distinctions between these two aspects. Both phases are connected to the primary accounting system, however inventory management usually provides information on the movement of inventory while the inventory valuation techniques differ from the inventory management.

Inventory valuation encompasses all methods that aid in the costing of the inventory as well as any adjustment to the value of the specific inventory. With advanced knowledge and methods you'll be able to know how the valuation methods can cause major changes in the profits of your company.

Because you are the one getting familiar with how to use and access the features and tools for valuationWe will then discuss the specifics of the changes in the profitability.

FIFO Evaluation

The FIFO technique is a method of valuation or method designed to take into account the actual cost of inventory. FIFO generally means "FIRST IN FIRST out" that means any item that is bought or purchased first will be first to be sold. The majority of experts and advanced users adhere to FIFO valuation techniques, in which the items are in a small quantity and are able to be identified separately.

It is important to know that all items need to be identified separately and appraised in a reasonable manner in order for FIFO in order to provide accurate valuations of inventory. In QuickBooks this feature lets you set the whole inventory valuation record and management records in accordance with this method. Be aware that valuation techniques integrate with the methods of managing inventory since valuation serves as the basis for the inventory being controlled.

The first thing you'll need to do is allow your FIFO valuation method within QuickBooks to allow you to do the valuation of your items.

I. Navigate to Files, Preferences> Items and Inventory.

ii. When you have clicked in the Advanced Settings button then navigate into the FIFO tab. It is inside the advanced settings screen.

iii. Check the box that indicates use FIFO then choose the date that you will start from the time you wish to have FIFO valuation of your inventory.

iv. Enter two times in order to store the modifications, and to go back on the QuickBooks interface.

If you're just installing the advanced interface for QuickBooks and haven't previously utilized QuickBooks, then each item that you'll include will automatically considered to be as a FIFO appraisal method. However, if you've recently made the decision to switch from the method you are currently using to FIFO in the company's files, then a portion of your reports may be affected.

The most common reports that will affect this modification are the financial statement, also known as the position , also known as the balance sheet, inventories valuation sheets, as well as the loss and profit report, which will include the price of the goods sold. The value and amounts of the figures that are reported in each report will be adjusted according to the FIFO valuation.

It is evident that fundamental principle for this FIFO technique is the fact that all of your inventory, that is purchased first is sold first and the price will be the same. The major difference with this method is that items with significant value that are bought later will appear for a short time on the systems and sheets since the older inventory will be removed from your inventory lists.

But, QuickBooks still shows the average value for each inventory item irrespective of the method you choose to use. However, when creating the reports the method that you have set in your settings will be automatically followed by QuickBooks. In default, the standard inventory valuation method is utilized to calculate the profit however, once FIFO valuation option is turned on all reports will be created by utilizing FIFO.

Adjusting the Values of the Inventory

There are times when your stock might be subject to certain damage that could result in the item becoming damaged to a certain extent or even completely or beyond repair. In these situations, QuickBooks allows you and its users to make changes to inventory quickly, ensuring you can ensure that the accounting data is accurate.

These adjustments can be made by calculating the amount of remaining inventory or on the amount of inventory. The primary reasons behind these adjustments are usually identified following the stock count which the manager or you will carry out.

I. Go to the Home icon in the Icon Bar and then select it.

ii. You can go in the Company section located on the right-hand side of your Home Window.

iii. Select Inventory Activities -> Change Quantity/Value on Hand.

iv. You must enter the type of adjustment you wish to implement into the inventory sheet. Select the inventory that you would like to make adjustments to.

. After you have adjusted either the amount or quantity of stock, hit Enter to save your change to your company's file.

Remember that when you have adjusted your inventory within your accounts the double entry is automatically generated by QuickBooks. This will take into account any type of change and then pass the Journal entry dependent on the variable change. For example, if you modify the quantity of inventory you have and then reduce it, QuickBooks will be able to determine the loss to be a result and pass the Journal entry to reflect it.

If, however, you show an improvement in value your inventory, QuickBooks will view this as an increase for the business. You must ensure that the methods you use to value inventory are in line with the adjustments to inventory that you'll integrate. If not, your financials may be affected by net profitability.

The adjustments to inventory will be automatically performed its duties based on the current valuation method as well as the method of managing inventory. Therefore, you do not have to worry about inconsistencies which can arise from these kinds of adjustments.

Chapter 3: Incorporating The Inventory

Many corporations around the world split their part of their work into different segments. Certain of them buy the raw materials to create specific items for a final product. Others assemble these specific units and then offer them to the market. However, other companies purchase the finished products in bulk from assembly units and then sell them to dealers or to retailers.

In these situations, the inventory is the final form of the product and is sold in the market. Sometimes, the inventory needs to be reassembled with other components for it to function properly. In either scenario you'll find that QuickBooks takes into account the particular requirements of its customers in the most advanced capabilities.

The assembly tool that you can use for inventory can be a huge benefit to those who are creating your inventory into products you want to sell. The features for assembly have advantages.

* It brings together the various products and their prices to make an all-in-one product.

* It also permits you to charge expenses, such as wage and salary which are directly related to the product that is paid to the final product.

* You can also incorporate certain overhead costs or non-inventory services to the process of assembling.

This gives you a lot of benefits of combining every variable to calculate the cost of the final product. With the cost of services and other costs being included in the price in assembly. This gives you with an accurate estimate of the total cost of the product.

You can get access to this tool via:

I. clicking on the Inventory Activities tab within the Company section of the Home window.

ii. Select the option to build Assemblies.

iii. Choose the product you would like to put together and enter the number of finished products you would like to receive.

iv. Once you've entered the desired number of units to build, click enter to Build and close.

You can also activate the reminder in the event that you are getting low on stock by going to Company> Reminder. You can also build an individual list of items and items that must be purchased by you to be incorporated to create your final item. Choose"Add New option from the Builder Assemblies window to design your own product.

Are there situations where you can't use the Inventory Assembly tool won't be useful?

There is a small drawback of this feature, which is that it's not advised for large manufacturing units that have multiple stages of production for the final product. This is typically the case for items that are component of mass-production.

The reason is that, during regular production there will be likely to be some typical loss or gain. The gains or losses cannot be easily adjusted across the whole batch of products made. Therefore, the margins of gains or losses becomes more difficult to adjust because the amount or value of the finished goods or the whole lot isn't quantified per unit.

There's a solution to this issue. If you are in control over the inventory utilized in the assembly process and the price per hour for labors and overheads is clear and you are able to determine the cost of the final products when the time is up in the whole amount.

In a situation that is always at a rapid pace as well as it is the JIT (Just within time) supply and delivery system is being followed, then this feature won't benefit you. Instead, it could create a rift in your business operations.

It is essential to analyze your own system to determine if these tools will or do not be beneficial to you.

Pro Tips to Handle your Inventory Records

Advanced inventory tools, features and methods of QuickBooks might seem interesting and relevant but it is important to keep an eye on the effects that your inventory has on your reporting requirements.

If you run retail businesses, then it is recommended to utilize the FIFO valuation method using the barcode feature and multi-scanning capabilities. Most times the technique of valuation can assist in understanding the latest costs of your product, which allows you to ensure that your profit margins are accurate.

If you choose to use the weighted-average method to measure your inventory, it will cause recent price hikes to be compared with the products you bought earlier. This will have a major impact on your income and loss statement because it will raise the price of selling goods and lower the profit.

* If your business's operations include selling water, petroleum or other liquid products exclusively, then you must apply the default weighted average method using methods for adjusting inventory. This is because such products and inventory tend to be in sync with market prices. Therefore, it can ensure an improved management, with a decrease in price of selling.

FIFO valuation techniques aren't effective in these scenarios because it's difficult to track the inventory that is purchased and then sold. For example, oil tankers have mixed oil within their containment units. And should you ever receive your inventory from your customers, you will not be able distinguish the inventory according to FIFO.

* Inventory assemblies operate in direct alignment in direct correlation with FIFO appraisal method. Therefore, a more effective cost analysis could be conducted based on the FIFO valuation, rather than the weighted average method of valuation. This allows you to determine the proper cost that is being charged to final product.

Typically, businesses employ the weighted average approach, however it's not a great option in the event of an unexpected price increase or when there are lots of normal losses or gains throughout the production.

Therefore, you should be well-aware of the methods and tools you'll use to manage your inventory appraisal, valuation, and adjustment. Each tool or technique is designed to serve optimally when used in conjunction with another method, tool or technique.

Advanced Lists of Services

A lot of businesses do not rely on the products or services to generate income by selling it on the marketplace. They offer services to keep their functioning. There is a chance that your business may offer any kind of service. For example, you could market an air conditioner and simultaneously providing maintenance services for the air conditioner that you sold.

Another scenario is that you provide an advisory or reservation service to your client. Whatever the case, you'll need to establish an advanced system to manage your services, and make sure that all of your services are paid on time. The proper usage of advanced billing and invoicing processes will be covered in a subsequent chapter.

Utilizing billing rate lists to help with advanced configuration

The most popular usage of advanced billing rate lists can be found in law firms, consultancy firms, or marketing and software companies. These lists of billing rates provide the prices of how your client will be charged according to the type of person they seek their advice.

In law firms there are managers, partners and even trainees who provide legal advice and counsel for their customers. The current situation is that the price of legal consultation for an apprentice or trainee will be lower than that of the partner in the firm. That means every individual within the company would be charged an individual billing rate which would be paid to the client when they require consultancy.

Additionally, the same person could offer different types of advice or kinds of consultancy. For example, for an opinion on legal matters the trainee could cost $20 or $30, when if the trainee offers corporate consultation it could cost between $40 and $50.

In these situations such cases, a correct billing rate list should be prepared in order to make sure that the customer is properly charged and not overly in any way for any particular service.

i. Select List > Billing rate list from the menu bar.

ii. Select the options of activities and choose the new ones.

iii. You will be able to select an option for fixed rates or an option for a custom rate. Choose the one you prefer and the option to create custom if you would like to include various billing rates for various services.

iv. Enter one time to save the modifications.

V. Go towards the Vendor center using the Vendor option in the bar menu.

vi. Select your desired vendor/ trainee/ apprentice/ manager/partner.

vii. Go to the tab for payment and then add the rate you want.

viii. Enter to save the changes.

After this has been completed once you have completed this, you'll be able to include the times of the relevant vendors to the timesheet, that can be done manually or by using an automated system. This allows the expenses for the suppliers to be billed directly when the client is invoiced. QuickBooks will generate separate records for each of the employees that will provide these services for their customers.

Chapter 4: Advance Cash Flow

Management and Sales

A company is in operating because of its capacity to earn income with every day. This, of course, helps the business expand, expand, and build an image of goodwill for its business. Every business is driven by one goal, and that is to boost its sales in order to increase the profits it earns. This is the most common method that is employed by many companies to gain access to the market that is not being explored or expand their market share across different areas.

The most important element is cash, which is what drives or encourages the business to increase its operations and grow to become a massive business. It is possible that companies have massive revenue turnovers each year, however the amount of profit that is passed down to them is nothing at the end

The reason for this is because these businesses do not evaluate their cash income for every sale. Certain businesses earn a great cash earnings on each sale, which is for each sale between $50 and they could earn between $10 and $5. This kind of cash income from such margins give the company the chance to expand into the market and increase market share.

At the final point, be aware that everything boils down to the relative prices and the price ranges that every company sets to ensure its margins are secure. Certain businesses have fixed price rates for all items give them the capacity to manage their business operations and ensure an ongoing flow of cash.

Beginning with Estimate Projections

One of the primary tasks that big companies undertake is the making of estimates and projections about an employment or contract before deciding to accept the contract. Also, you must be aware that the primary way of maintaining a positive financial balance in cash flows is knowing how much cash you'll receive in the event of a transaction.

This can be a result of a variety of elements like expenses, overheads, and any extra costs, etc. that you'll need to pay for to finish an order or complete a task. Estimates can also help you calculate the margins and rates that are required to control the other expenses. These additional costs can include marketing, administrative costs, and distribution costs, etc.

QuickBooks lets you easily create estimates, while providing the benefit of comparing the estimate to the actual expenses and actual revenue. In addition, QuickBooks also offers the most effective method of evaluating your estimates on the basis of sales prices or costs which were previously paid.

To prepare an estimate of the work:

i. Locate the Estimate icon, which is found on the Home.

ii. Select the correct job or the client from the drop-down list.

iii. The table in the following paragraphs, list all of the pertinent costs or items lists for the specific project or customer.

iv. Enter to save and end the browser.

After the customer or the client accepts the estimate and you are able charging the client on an agreement agreement. Clients will be charged every time you issue an invoice. It is the primary document used by the client to sign and send you the payment.

The Elegant Method of Invoicing

Large corporations adhere to a strict procedure to ensure that each business process is conducted with a clearly defined policy. These practices allow businesses to develop into independent organizations that can carry out their duties in a controlled environment. These kinds of practices result in advanced methods to deal with issues or an anomaly.

But, that does not mean that smaller-medium size businesses or entrepreneurs shouldn't be following these guidelines. The modern use of every function depends on the capability to integrate into the control system. Certain elements of businesses cannot be fully integrated into an automation system, but important activities can be accomplished as in modern day practices.

Similar to invoices. The majority of businesses invoicing their customers without preparing a prior draft of a bill which outlines the estimated cost of their project and projected revenue from a project. Large companies adhere to this model of invoices where they first present their estimate to their customers to ask them to take.

QuickBooks lets you easily make invoices from estimates that have been created. Invoicing is a process that follows the pattern that is followed by QuickBooks and fully defines the process using the aid of the flowchart that is on QuickBooks' home page.

I. Go to the home page and choose Create an invoice.

ii. Find the Job or Customer in the search results and then use the Arrow keys to move it upwards and downwards in on the drop-down menu. Use the tab keys to select the desired user or job.

iii. Select the estimate you want to invoice in the window for Estimates Available.

iv. Enter to create an create an invoice in accordance with the estimate.

If you're a contracting company and you follow the method of invoicing that is using the percent of completion or the progress completion If you do, you should utilize certain fields during the process of invoicing.

I. First, select"Progress Invoice" and select the desired percentage of the task's completion.

ii. Select any of the options available and then fill in the information to finish the invoice.

iii. Enter the code once you're completed with your bill.

This sophisticated method of invoicing will provide you with better control of cash flow throughout the course of the project. This will allows you to monitor the progress made. Not only that, it also lets you evaluate the estimates against the actual costs for the project to determine where the cost was costing you.

Utilizing the estimation and invoicing methods You will be able to:

Know precisely the stage within which your project completed.

Control your cash flows by analyzing invoices that you have sent to your customer.

Re-evaluate the risks to credit associated with specific customers in relation to the payment conditions.

* Re-assess the timeliness of completeness and timely delivery of your project client.

This will make your life easier by allowing you to effortlessly manage the many complex tasks while keeping overview of how your jobs or projects are being completed.

Eliminating redundant Sales Invoices and Orders

As the size of your business increases as you expand, more and more problems begin to surface in the course of time. The most significant issue that businesses have to deal with is the provision of inefficient inventory or items to the client. While it may seem easy to solve there is a more complicated issue on a larger size or even a mid-sized company.

For instance, a client has requested certain items to be delivered to them in a specified period of time according to the terms of the contract. Your logistics department will deliver certain items to that customer in accordance with the sales order specified in the contract. If there's no way to keep tracking of which products or inventory has been shipped out for the client, this could result in the following problems:

* You'll end up sending more items to the client that are not required by them.

* You'll lose the cash you have earned since the inventory will shrink. inventory that is in the inventory.

* This could result in a gap between the supply and demand chain of your company's operations that will cause you to lose goodwill.

To address this problem, QuickBooks provides the full record of the items that were sent to the customer , based upon the delivery that was partial. This lets you to see the amount of goods that were delivered at the request of the client. This tracking mechanism works in accordance with the purchase order.

If the purchase order is fully satisfied, then a final invoice will be issued. However, if there are several partial deliveries, the invoice can also be invoiced according to the partial deliveries made at the time.

I. You can go to the Homepage and click on the Sales Order icon that is located in the home screen.

ii. Select a specific customer, or a specific job against the sales order that is to be made.

iii. Create the sales invoice and complete the necessary information about the purchase.

iv. When the items are delivered during each stage in the delivery in the sales order, enter the total amount of products that are delivered on your sales invoice.

V. Press enter to save the modifications.

This will automatically update your invoice, and permit you to invoice your customer based on the product partially delivered. You must select the same job or customer in the invoice creation window in order to create an invoice, and QuickBooks will fill in all the details, as well as the products that are delivered directly to your customer.

You'll be able to control completely and access the system for goods dispatch to limit the possibility of your customer being undersupplied. Also, it will ensure that the invoicing process and the billing process will function efficiently together with the distribution system fully integrated into the system. Through keeping a proper record of and documentation of the products that are delivered it will ensure that there are no duplicates in the processes.

If there are several sales orders from a certain customer, these can be merged into one invoice. All you need to do is choose any of the wanted several sales orders to be combined into one invoice. This will generate an invoice that has a final amount that is due to your customer.

Benefits of reviewing sales orders

Sometimes, you're too busy to realize that some of the sales orders for one specific customer are not completely completed. In this case, for instance, you might have received numerous sales orders from various customers, and then you provided one customer with a part of their products due to the lack of inventory in your warehouse.

In these instances it could damage your goodwill and put your reputation at risk because when a customer is not satisfied by your service the customer may not purchase another time from your company. In turn, this could damage your reputation on the market.

But, you can make sure that you aren't doing this by looking over your sales orders that are open from time to time to determine the customer who didn't get any items or got the goods in part. The report feature of QuickBooks permits you to quickly access this feature that assures that all business operations are completed on a timely basis.

I. Open and navigate Reports > Sales> Open Sales Order by Client using the bar menu.

ii. You can modify and filter the report by clicking the sales Order by Item option in the menu. You can also select the Customize Report option to choose the fields you want to filter and choose filters.

You can also modify the sales order report to suit various ways to give you the information you require.

This method also permits you to check your cash flow with each purchase. The most significant issue you may encounter is cash management which is when you are required to pay , and when it is necessary to get the cash. Sales order reports let you analyze the demand on a regular basis, which when taken together and the flow of cash each month, will permit you to invest any additional cash to cover any cash shortage flow.

i. Take the Open Sales order report for the Customer from the Reports menu bar.

ii. Get the report about the inventory-in-hand at that date.

iii. Create an Excel file using an Excel file that contains the Sales Order Report and rank each customer according to the terms of their payment, i.e., customers who will pay the earliest to be ranked first , and the same for others.

iv. Combine the inventory at hand report and the Excel file and assign the inventory to each of the open sales order from the top-ranked customer, starting with the first.

In this way, you'll be able determine whether you'd have enough stocks in order to meet the demands or if you'll need to purchase more stock to meet the demand. Also when you find out in the report that you have plenty of stock and are likely to receive cash in a short time in addition, the best approach to manage the cash surplus is by investing it in short-term deposit or bonds that provide the possibility of earning interest.

This kind of sophisticated analytical analysis can help you to control your finances and sales demands in a more effective and the most efficient way.

Chapter 5: Sales And Cost Management Systems

The most common issue you may encounter is changing the cost and costs of every product or item. The other side of the coin is another issue is the creation of various prices for different customer levels. As an example, it is possible that you could need the system to make sales invoices for wholesalers in a different way from that of your regular retailers, or you could wish that certain customers receive a discount above market in exchange for their long-term loyalty or confidence.

There is an approach to handle all of these issues all at once? Are there ways you can deal with this problem? Yes, there is, and that is through the Cost and sales management systems. But, it is important to be aware that there isn't similar system within QuickBooks and it is not an exclusive tool. It's basically a mix of various techniques and tools being used to create a more advanced view.

The greatest benefits and usage of the cost and sales management system can only be realized when they are properly used to coordinate. By updating the standard cost of each of the inventory items, you'll be able save more time, and also increase flexibility in managing the operational system.

Additionally, when the prices of your specific product are modified, they will automatically update the selling prices for each item. This process is able to be completed efficiently and effectively with a clearly defined set of guidelines when you are able to easily alter the specific markup or profit margin in addition to the revised costs. This is possible through two distinct functions. One is cost levels, while another is the markup of the price that the merchandise.

The price levels automatically regulate the cost of the inventory and the sales price of the inventory could be either fixed at a certain percentage of expense or an adjustable percentage based on the client or specific product. This allows you to conduct more thorough analysis of profitability and to visualize the actual revenue made from selling every inventory item.

In contrast, the markup represents the cost of finance or profit for late payments or a set percentage that is added to the final price of the bill of customers.

These price levels need to be activated first before you to be able to utilize these prices.

I. Navigate to Edits> Preferences > Sales & Customers icon or option to select it.

ii. Select the tab Company preferences and then tick the option to use price levels.

iii. Enter to save the modifications.

When these price levels are set, you can alter and use them for each and every item. Go to the Lists option on the menu bar and when you have selected prices, you are able to set them up according to your preferences. The prices are assigned to customers through their Customer Center.

It is important to note that you may alter the rates when you invoice your customers. Therefore, once you assign the appropriate price levels to different customers, invoices will use the rates you have set as per the current prices.

Innovative Steps to Keep the Sales Transactions under control

So, how do you create an advanced system to simplify and manage the tasks? Are there ways to combine the various processes and use them all simultaneously as my needs increase? In this moment you may be asking similar or different concerns that are popping up in your head.

The most frequently asked issue is just how far this system for managing sales transactions actually get. To answer this query, let's consider an example. Imagine that your business's operations are more complicated than was originally thought. This is the reason why you're looking to establish an organized and consistent policy and procedure in order to manage your daily business operations.

Of course, the primary and most significant issue that will arise is managing sales orders. At some moment, you'll have to handle multiple sales orders, while in the opposite direction you'll need to contact customers who haven't made their payments. Another common problem is managing invoices as well as stopping inventory supply to customers who have exceeded their credit limit.

These issues and concerns might seem simple to solve however, when they need to be addressed within your QuickBooks software, things could be difficult. However it is necessary to examine if there are loopholes or bypasses that could disrupt the regular processing of QuickBooks.

Here are a few of the latest techniques to handle your company's finance and sales.

1). Define specific credit risks for the most important customers.

Start by identifying your major customers for your company. These customers are essential sources for managing your business operations and ensuring that you make sales every month. They are in essence the long-term assets of your company to expand and continue to improve in the coming months or even years.

Recognizing the major customers and the emergence of credit risk that is variable with them will allow you to create the work to be more prioritized to ensure that they aren't dissatisfied with your products or services. Additionally it ensures that the customers won't create an issue with your company.

Be sure to have the right information for these customers. Major customers typically contribute approximately 15 percent of your revenue. Choose the proper amount of credit limit within

Customers > Customer Center> Edit the Payment Terms section in the Menu Bar. In addition, you can define the payment terms and whether the customer is able to avail the discount that is offered.

Additionally you should also set the proper price levels for these important customers, so that they can also to enjoy a variety of benefits working with your company. The setting of prices and credit limits for major customers will enable you to build an automated system to generate invoices and sales orders according to the agreed rates.

2). Make sure you have a good job description and estimate the amount

It is vital that, before you start your project by creating estimates or distributing the quotation to your customer You have all the fields that are pre-defined for your customers to be able to communicate with them effectively.

A budget can help you decide whether providing products or services over a long period can be beneficial to the company or not. Customers with large amounts of business should receive an appropriate estimate to ensure they agree with the bill and continue to use your products or services.

Poor negotiations could result in you ending having to pay funds or cause unclarity with your clients. When you are preparing your estimated bill make sure you include overhead costs and other costs that are associated with it in order to inquire of the client if they'll be reimbursed for such expenses.

Also, make sure that you have put in place the markups in the event of late payments by customers. If you believe that the customer to be in good financial standing and wish to establish long-term business relationships do not include the markup for late payments.

3). Update the sales order

The most effective way to adhere to the sophisticated mechanism is to create an order for sales every time important customers place an order to deliver. This will allow you to keep an eye on both your inventory and the delivery of the items to the buyer. This has been discussed previously.

It is important to ensure that your sales orders are made according to the estimate bill in order to control the flow of cash in accordance with the estimated bill. In the event that there is a difference in the sales order it is easy to reconcile it to the estimated bill to learn the source of any issues or errors.

This process will make sure that your main customer does not be able to complain about any issue that occurs during the course of work.

4). Generating invoices

When it comes to invoicing the process will differ for large customers. When an invoice is prepared, the details is automatically entered specific to the customer. If the customer is not able to pay any previous charges and is in excess of the amount of credit allowed, QuickBooks will automatically create the invoice, but it will show the warning message.

This will facilitate a more efficient procedure and allow you to get confirmation that the customer has received the outstanding balance due and the invoices.

Then, you'll be able to decide on whether you would like to keep supplying inventory to the client and let the customer pay off the debt at a later time. You may also choose to deliver the goods once the dues have been paid. In any situation, the actual work is at this point and you'll be required to make a decision.

The entire procedures and methods have enabled you to regulate the continuous flow of cash and income into your company. Of of course, it will be your decision if you'd prefer to adhere to an entirely different set of processes.

These steps will ensure:

* Your top customers and the principal business incomes are automatically analyzed and monitored.

You are able to regulate the entire revenue cycle and evaluate it against estimations and expectations.

* You can manage and manage inventory based on demand from customers and the annual demands of all of your customers.

5). Performance tracking using the reports combined

It is also possible to create a variety of combined reports by combining the same or multiple reports. As mentioned earlier the combined reports assist you to analyze the issues in a clearer manner. If you're looking to determine how the amount of money due to the customer affects the business's operations, you can get two reports.

A report that provides an analysis of the aging of the customer , and another report will show the loss of cash reserves each month. When you put both reports, you'll be able better assess the extent of the impact the time delay in payment from the client that is affecting business.

With this approach it is also possible to be able to evaluate your cash reserves to the receivables total at the time of a specific date. There's a method to establish the amount of receivables you are able to allow for all customers at any time.

To determine the minimum amount of your total receivables you could compare it with the amount of your payments to your suppliers. If your receivables exceed 50% higher than your payables, it indicates that you have a suitable minimum amount to keep on your account receivables.

To determine the maximum amount of your total receivables you need to compare it to your cash reserves. When your reserves of cash are 50percent more than the receivables, this indicates that in the event that the customer fails to pay but you are still capable of paying back the supplier and also order additional inventory to meet future needs.

You can also monitor the performance of various aspects of business, including the level of profitability and the amount that are saved by a specific project or contract. It is important to keep track of the amount of money received from customers as well as the invoices that are sent to them since when they fall behind at any point they could trigger a serious disruption in the flow of cash and managing cash flows.

Make sure you watch out for major customers. QuickBooks offers a range of reports that are combined. Additionally, you can utilize reports like the Budget vs. Actual Report found in Reports under budgets as well as Forecasts to determine the amount of variance that exists between the budgeted numbers and the actual numbers. This will help you find certain flaws in your budget that you may not have considered for when you made a budget.

Budgets are a great method of monitoring your company's performance and turnover. Not only that, they can also determine the various goals and the chances of reaching of these targets over the medium, short and long-term. If you want to make use of this technique, make sure to begin by creating a budget for the client to be able to compare the numbers later.

6). Establishing security roles

Another method to ensure there's no collusion within your business operations is making security roles available in QuickBooks and checking them periodically from time intervals. Each time someone connect into the QuickBooks system an audit trail will be generated that will record the modifications created by users.

Audit trails are accessible through the Reports > Accountants & Taxes choice in the menu. Audit trails are the complete history of each person's activities within QuickBooks. With the feature you will be able to be able to fully investigate the person accountable in breaching the rules or for being involved in illegal activities.

This means you can be sure that fake invoices and counterfeit sales orders don't get ever generated.

If you follow these steps by following these steps, you will reduce the possibility of having any kind of inconsistent or other error that could occur. In addition, this whole procedure will allow you to:

* To keep track of any transactions you might not have entered to the computer system.

* To analyze the operations of the company to verify the company's ability to operate in the coming years.

Chapter 6: Recovering Debts Of Customers

Sometimes, customers do not pay the invoice you've sent them. In general, it's difficult to track every customer's outstanding invoice. Because of this, QuickBooks offers the ability to keep track of all open invoices which have not yet already been settled by the client.

QuickBooks comes with a reminder function in addition to a reminder feature that is found in the upper left corner of the screen. This feature shows all invoices that are due and the due payments that must be paid to suppliers. This feature lets you assess any penalties to your client for making payments late, and also protects you from having to pay any charges to your suppliers due to late payments.

You can also view all open invoices by clicking the Reports > Customers and Receivables collection report option on the menu bar. It will show the complete list of customers who haven't paid their outstanding debts.

Additionally, you can also send the customers you've selected a fair notice about their outstanding balances via the Customer Center. After selecting the Collection Letters option, you can select your clients to whom you would like to mail the letters. It is possible to choose the pre-designed format provided by QuickBooks or add a template that you have created in QuickBooks to highlight any outstanding balances.

All of these are standard features in QuickBooks that do not require any kind of activation. The only difference is that Collection Center is not enabled until you start using QuickBooks.

I. Navigate to Edit , then choose the Preferences.

ii. After you click on the Sales & Customers, navigate to the tab Company Preferences.

iii. Check the box that says Enable Collection centre.

iv. Press Enter one time to save any changes you have made.

It is then easy to navigate to the Collection Center within The Customer Center. QuickBooks will display all outstanding or late invoices, along with any other invoices that are due.

Invoicing all your customers simultaneously

One of the top time savings tools offered by QuickBooks includes the batch invoice tool, which assists you by creating invoices for a variety of customers simultaneously. This helps accelerate the process of billing your customers as well as keeping record of all sales income.

i. You can access the Customer -and then the Create batch invoices by clicking on the bar menu.

ii. Add all customers you want to invoicing by choosing them from the search box.

iii. Press Enter to open the following window.

iv. Incorporate all of the products you would like to invoice your customers for.

V. Press enter twice to create invoices, and let QuickBooks finish entering the transaction.

You may also choose to print the batch invoice that was prepared, or send them to your customers. Before sending the invoice at your clients, be sure the email addresses of your customers are listed in their details tabs.

Advanced Reimbursable Costs for Reimbursable Costs

In many service sectors there are some expenses that have to be to be borne, specifically for client's needs, can be reimbursed. For example when a members of the audit team visits the client to consult, and then charges for the journey to the office of the client their own premises. In such instances, the expenses are to be recouped from the client.

Many clients frequently request their lawyers or their consultants to meet with them at the office for some advice or other reasons. So, any costs paid by the consultant need to be billed to the customer in the final bill. Sometimes, these expenses comprise the third party that was present before the customer or client for your company.

So, you are able to be able to charge these costs to the customer on their invoices by choosing one particular customer.

I. Click on it. Click on the Enter Bills icon on the home page. Add all bills or expenses that relate to the customer.

ii. Include all bills as well as the descriptions of them (if you've already completed this, then move onto the next stage).

iii. Enter the name of the customer on the Field for Customer Jobs, and mark the checkbox that reads, "Billable?"

iv. Enter to save all bills.

V. Go to the Create invoice icon on the main page, and then select the customer you want to invoice.

vi. When you click on the customer the pop-up window will pop-up.

vii. Choose the option that reads, "Select the outstanding billable cost and time to add to the invoice."

viii. Add up all the expenses such as time, costs, and fees that are incurred against the customer.

ix. Add the amount of Markup or percentage if you want.

x. Press Enter to include all charges

xi. Close and save the invoiceonce you're done.

You can also include expenses for payroll that will be charged to the customer on their invoices by selecting the billable option near the bottom of the sheet for payroll.

This feature lets you segregate all costs that do not relate to your company or have been paid by your company for the benefit of the client. The reimbursable expenses are included as part of your invoices and appear as receivables on your balance statements.

It is also possible to view all the expenses and time not billed to the customer through the Reports tab -> Customers and Receivables Unbilled Costs by Job. In keeping records of all non-billed costs, you'll easily be able to modify your financial records.

This feature can be beneficial to you because:

* Sifting incremental costs for each job. This allows you to see the real price of your product or service quickly.

Adjusting the amount of invoices to ensure that all reimbursable expenses and the time is paid to the customer.

• Reviewing each month at ending about any outstanding not yet billed charges or time which is not being charged to the client.

Innovative Mechanism to Handle Sales Tax

Certain situations are required to charge multiple sales tax on the client to purchase different products. In most cases, the details of sales tax for the particular customer is recorded when the newly added customer's name is entered into the database. However, that's the general details about sales tax.

The sales tax we're talking about is the tax you pay on products you buy. In the case of cotton or steel to your customers There is an opportunity you'll find that your tax rates for steel might be different. However the tax rate for cotton might be different. For instance, if you're offering services or selling products.

In addition, there are times you will also find prices for specific products, while for certain items there is an exact amount you must pay. The best method to deal with such circumstances is to add a distinct sales tax rates on a single invoice.

1. The preparation of the items to be sold tax

I. Go to the List by using the menu bar and select the option to list items.

ii. Right-click on the window and select the new option.

iii. Select the Sales tax that is applicable to the item type.

iv. Complete all of the necessary details that will appear within the windows.

V. Enter to save the file as well as close the windows.

vi. Repeat these steps in case it is required.

2. In preparation of an item for sub-total

i. After selecting the list via the menu, and then selecting the option that is new, select the the drop-down menu that reads "Subtotal."

ii. Complete the required fields and then press Enter in order to save your item.

3. Invoice the sales tax in multiple installments on the invoice

i. You must ensure that the tax rate for new tax items will be zero percent.

ii. Select the sales tax option at the the bottom line of your invoice.

iii. Include all items that are taxed at the individual specified rates and be included within the statement.

iv. After selecting each tax item, you must include in the total item.

V. Charge the sales tax you want to charge under the subtotal item to determine the tax due on that subtotaled value.

vi. Include any non-taxable item following the tax on sales to add to your invoice.

vii. Enter to save the invoice then close your invoice.

If you charged an wrong sales tax on your client or client, you can delete an invoice to issue brand new invoice for sales tax. If the payment was cleared and the client has had paid the sales tax then you may give a refund of overcharge as well as issue a credit note or adjust the amount that was overpaid later on using the subsequent invoices issued by the clients.

QuickBooks also alters the sales tax of the invoices if you issue an credit note to the customer. This allows both you and your client to report this change to the tax authorities.

i. Select Customers, then Create Credit Memosor Refunds from the menu.

ii. Input the customer's name in the drop-down menu. (Note you will not be able to issue a credit note to a third-party that is not identified because QuickBooks requires that you include the name of the customer).

iii. Include all the items which you received the package back from the client.

iv. Make sure you include only those items that are tax-deductible in the field and then add their tax rates as per the individual.

V. Then, add the sum of the amount to determine the subtotaled value of the items.

vi. Input your tax rate of choice after the subtotal amount.

vii. Press Enter the number vii. Press enter to Save & Close the invoice.

Adjusting Prepayments and Advances Invoices

As a standard practice clients are required to make an advance payment to secure their order the need arises to purchase many stocks.

Additionally, certain businesses demand the advance amount of a specific percentage is deposited prior to the beginning of work or on a project that will be adjusted based on the invoice at the end.

This practice is largely practiced by service companies which involve consultants and contractors who require their clients to pay a certain amount prior to beginning work in the course of the work.

There is a chance that you will confront a situation in which you'll need to ask the customer to make an advance prior to delivering the products or provide the services. QuickBooks can assist you with the process of adjusting these types of advances received from the clients. In addition, QuickBooks shows all advances or adjustments that are currently pending against the invoices of a specific client.

1. Receiving Cash Advance

I. Select the Receive Payments icons from the home page.

ii. Choose the preferred customer along with the amount as well as the method of payment for the advance.

iii. In the lower left corner the new options will be listed, with the payment being described in the form of "Overpayment."

iv. Select the Leave credits that can be used in the future to earn an account for customer.

V. Press enter to Save and Close.

After you've completed the process your work, the balance of the customer's account will appear as an amount that is negative on the receivables aspect. You can then modify this advance using the invoices you have sent by the client.

2. Adjusting the advance

i. Select to click on the Create Invoice icon from the homepage and then select the specific customer with advance readily available.

ii. After you've created an invoice, choose the Apply Credits button.

iii. The new screen will appear with the progress against the specific customer.

iv. Choose the credit you wish to use as well as the amount you want to adjust to the amount of your invoice. You have the option of making a complete adjustment , or partial adjustments to the invoice.

V. Press enter to apply the modifications.

vi. Enter again to save to close your invoice.

You can view the reports that show the balances outstanding of customers as negative and depict the balance as an advance. Remember that your accounts receivables must not show an account with a negative balance by year's end. In the event of a negative balance, the auditors or the authorities could ask questions about the balance that remains.

The best method to make sure that the balances for the year are also adjusted is to pass an adjustment entry that removes the balance negative of the customer's accounts receivable, and then transfers the balance to an account of liability for that customer.

The balances can be adjusted, while also ensuring that there isn't any breach of accounting rules. It is possible to reclassify or adjust the balances following the year's end by reversing identical entries. When you're within the General Journal, select the option to reverse transactions and highlight the one you want to reverse.

But, you could use a different method and process that creates the liability account for the client from the very beginning. After you receive the money from the client it is easy to change accounts to the liability one you created for the client.

This means that there is no need to change your balances when the year comes to an end and you won't be concerned about breaking any laws or standards. The remaining procedures and steps will be carried out in the same way as previously described, with no need for any modifications. However, you should ensure that each time you send an invoice, the invoice needs to be adjusted in relation to the advance amount or be adjusted to an additional balance in the future.

Chapter 7: Closes Off Accounts Of Customers

With Bad Debt

In very rare situations you might find out that your client won't be able to settle the amount due to you because they've declared bankruptcy. These kinds of cases aren't typically seen as part of normal business transactions. If you're a stable profitable business and you discover the fact that one of your smaller clients has declared bankruptcy, it won't have a significant impact on your business.

If one of your customers, which is a significant portion of your earnings within your company, declares bankruptcy, you could face a dreadful outcome. One of the consequences is the loss of huge revenue and cash out of the system. When you lose customers, it could put at risk not just the receivables, but also on the future earnings that were to be recouped by the client.

In the event that you write off debts that are not paid for these customers could cause a massive loss of cash and revenue but accounting of this type of transaction remains necessary. There are many options to alter the bad debts within

QuickBooks however the most commonly used method users use is the discount Allowed option.

With the discount permitted method, the outstanding balances are completely adjusted to the discount. This makes it very simple and flexible to utilize. But, this method doesn't account for the sales tax added to the invoices that were sent to the client.

Therefore, the other method, which very few people employ, is credit memos. Credit memos usually emphasize the tax reduction which is then written off in a direct manner. This method requires several adjustments and modifications because when it is issued a credit note you're increasing the inventory you have.

Let's suppose that you have lost both the inventory and revenues from the customer; in this case the credit memo will only be adjusted to reflect the loss in revenue as well as sales tax however, it will not adjust the inventory which has been incorporated into the business. In order to make adjustments, another entry needs to be made, in which the inventory will be modified or written off.

It is important to remember that even if you write-off the inventory in your account however, you'll still incur a loss to the accounts, that is not correct. If you write-off your inventory, you're creating the identical entry twice. Make sure that, when you make the account for bad debts, your sales cost or purchases aren't affected by the entry. So, your purchases or inventory could be written off in the future.

Also, keep in mind that you'll have to classify the entry after the year's end to demonstrate that the loss in revenue was due to the bad credit.

1. Writing off bad debts with the Discount permitted method

I. Go to your Receive Payments icon on the home screen and choose the icon.

ii. Select the customer with the balance you would like to deduct.

iii. Select the invoice that you wish to write off, and then choose the discount & Credit option.

iv. Add the total amount of the invoice in Discount Allowed.

V. Enter after you're done saving and Close.

In this way you are able to select the account with bad debt as the account that is allowed to discount. This way you will not have to make any inventory adjustments or reclassification adjustments.

2. Utilizing this method, you can use the Bad debt item to write off bad debts

This process is somewhat difficult, but if you can execute it correctly then you'll be able to alter all your balances of your account effortlessly. It involves three steps:

* Making an bad debt item that will be charged to the balance in a direct way as an expense.

• Preparing the credit note on the base of the item.

* Utilizing the credits from the Receive Payments window.

After you have completed all three phases, you'll be able to alter the balances on the accounts of customers based on the credit memos they have received. Additionally the sales taxes that are on invoices will be changed or reversed.

a. Making the bad debt on the list of items

I. Navigate to Item Lists in the menu bar located at the top.

ii. Right-click anywhere to select the new option.

iii. Choose the Other Charge option in the list , and continue to fill in the required information.

iv. Be sure to label the item Bad debt, and then select the account with bad debt for it.

V. Press enter to save the modifications and to create the item.

b. issuing the credit note to the bad debt customer

i. After clicking on the Refunds & Credits on the Home page, click on the desired customer to whom you'll issue a credit for bad debt memo.

ii. Choose the item of bad debt in the line, and then enter the item against which you're generating this bad loan.

iii. Input the total amount the bad debt that you wish to write off on the remaining balance.

iv. Complete the rest of the details, including the tax code and any tax that was imposed earlier, as well as any other details on the memo of credit.

V. Once you've done that, click"Apply to invoice" to generate the credit.

vi. Enter to save the changes and end the change.

C. Automatically apply the credit in the event of payments.

i. Simply select the customer in The Receive Payments symbol and then apply credits to reduce the balance completely.

ii. Once you've completed the process pressing enter, you will make the change permanent.

It is important to note that these strategies are employed to alter the principal accounts of customers with in debt. If there are minor insufficient payments by the client it is easy to adjust the amount in the window for Receiving Payments.

Simply add the amount you have received and mark the balance as Write off if you're sure that the client won't be able to be able to pay the remainder. After you have selected that option QuickBooks is going to ask you for the write-off account to pay the remaining amount. Select the account you wish to use and then press Enter to save the adjustments.

Chapter 8: The History Of Quickbooks

QuickBooks was developed by Scott Cook and Tom Proulx in 1983.

In 2003, it started to grow into various sectors. In the years since, this application has seen the launch of various versions that aim to improve its performance to meet your requirements. The workflow process and reports are designed in accordance with specific industry standards and the application is smoother.

Through the years the software has gained entry into several international markets.

The advantages of Quickbooks

Data Migration:

The information in the accounting software are transferred seamlessly into the spreadsheet. This is a good option if you wish to keep financial data in the spreadsheet.

User-friendly:

The software's power makes every task easy to the end user. The most important thing is that the extensive features of the software will are designed to meet the needs of medium and small businesses demands.

Plain sailing:

It's easy to see the status of your company by using the software. Understanding how it functions is straightforward and simple to grasp. It also requires only a short amount of learning.

Bank Transactions:

Every business transaction is recorded in a transparent manner and the software keeps in the process of recording transactions related to commissions, wages and salary, as well as profits, expenses, etc.

Invoices Generation:

Simple generation of invoices using your tablets, smartphones and even your computer system

Tax Calculations:

The tax calculation feature in QB provides you with the ability to calculate taxes for your business in a timely, precise and efficient manner.

Business Projections:

The option of business projections included in QuickBooks aids users of QuickBooks in creating future projections. However when someone wants to produce reports on earnings, sales, or expenses it is easy to work out what they need to do with business projections.

Setting up Quickbooks

In order to begin making plans for to set up your QuickBooks system, it's ideal to start by asking the following questions:

* What does accounting do?

* What exactly do the accounting system do?

When you've mastered this concept at the beginning and you'll see that the QuickBooks setting up process will make much more sense.

What does accounting mean?

It is important to first understand the basics of accounting. There is a lot of debate about the smallest specifics, but the majority would believe that accounting accomplishes four things that are important:

* Determines the amount of profit and loss.

* Reports on the financial situation of a company (its capital, assets and liabilities as well as net worth)

* Provides complete records of the liabilities, assets and equity accounts of the owner.

* Provides financial data to the stakeholders, particularly to management

What accounting systems are used?

Then take a glance at the various accounting systems can do, or at the very least, what small-scale business accounting systemsgenerally do:

• Prepare financial statements, such as balance sheets, income statements and other accounting reports.

Create business forms like check, pay checks, invoices customer statements and more.

Maintain detailed notes of the crucial accounts, including cash the accounts payable (amounts which customers have to pay to a company) and accounts payable (amounts due to a company its suppliers) inventories, fixed assets and so on.

* Perform tasks related to information management. For instance in the publishing sector book publishers usually give authors royalties. Therefore, it is a job that book publishers' accounting systems are required to perform.

WHAT QUICKBOOKS DO

Once you have a better understanding of the nature of accounting and what systems for accounting typically accomplish, you will be able to see in a certain way the things that QuickBooks can do:

* Produces financial statements

* Creates a variety of commonly used business forms, such as check, paychecks, customer invoices, statements from customers credit memos, purchase orders.

* Maintains detailed notes of a small number of important accounts like cash, accounts receivables accounts payable, inventory with simple configurations

QuickBooks accomplishes all of four functions that you'd like an accounting program to accomplish. Take a look at the list with the prior list ("What accounting systems can do"). The only thing that Quickbook does not offer is that it doesn't offer particular accounting software. For instance, QuickBooks doesn't do royalty accounting as discussed in the previous instance.

QuickBooks offers businesses and users plenty of flexibility. In the previous scenario that a book publisher could complete the majority of the tasks it requires to do for royalty accounting using QuickBooks. The work of royalty accounting requires a little playing around with the process of creating QuickBooks.

Why should you use Quickbooks?

What QuickBooks does extremely well. We're not suggesting that you should never try or use the accounting capabilities of a smaller accounting software solution, but you should consider the possibility that QuickBooks will remain in use for an LONG, LONG time.

It's much more likely the accounting software that has 600 users, as an example is likely to be shut down instead of a product such as QuickBooks that has more than 2 million users.

Installing Quickbooks

It is possible to install QuickBooks exactly the same method as you would install any other software. How you install a software depends on the version of Microsoft Windows you're using. However, in general, the most recent editions of Microsoft Windows require that you put the QuickBooks CD in your DVD drive or CD drive. If you do the above, Windows looks at the QuickBooks CD and recognizes it as a disc that contains a brand new, yet-to-be-installed software application and begins the process of setting up it. QuickBooks software.

You don't have to do anything extra in order to set up QuickBooks. Follow the on-screen directions. It is typical by the prompt to input your installation code, or code. This code is located inside the QuickBooks packaging, usually on the reverse of the envelope the disc is packaged in.

The QuickBooks installation process might ask you to answer a few questions regarding the way you would like QuickBooks installed. Most of the time, you will prefer to follow the suggestions that are default. Also, QuickBooks may ask you whether it is able to create a new folder which you can install QuickBooks program files.

QuickBooks software files. If so you should select yes.

In the event that your particular version of Microsoft Windows doesn't recognize that you've put the QuickBooks CD inside the computer's DVD or CD drive, there are two options:

* You are able to sit and wait. If you do, Windows will recognize that you've put the QuickBooks CD in your DVD or CD drive. Then after a brief wait (even even though it seems to be a long time), Windows starts the process of installing the QuickBooks software.

You can force manually to install the QuickBooks software. Windows comes with a tool can be used to either install or remove new programs (unsurprisingly called"Add/Remove Programs Tool). In simple terms you just need to open the Control Panel window, click the Add/Remove Programs tool, then follow the instructions displayed on the screen for instructing Windows to install a program on the DVD or CD on the computer's DVD or CD drive.

QuickBooks functions as an accounting system for multiple users. This means that a variety of users are able to use QuickBooks. This means that the

QuickBooks database file -- the storage of all QuickBooks data -- usually is located on a centrally accessible PC or server. Users who wish to access this QuickBooks data file can simply install the QuickBooks software on their computer and then use the software to access centrally stored QuickBooks file data. It is important to have a different QuickBooks copy on each of the computers where the QuickBooks program is installed. You can also purchase multi-user versions of QuickBooks that allow you to install the QuickBooks software on up five computers. This is since you don't want to be into software pirateywhich is a crime in the event of accidentally installing QuickBooks in the wrong manner.

The bottom line is: You require a valid copy of QuickBooks for each machine where you install QuickBooks.

EasyStep INTERVIEW

Once you have installed QuickBooks it is time to conduct an interview in order to setup QuickBooks for your business's accounting. When you conduct an interview you are providing plenty of data to QuickBooks. Practically speaking it is essential to have you can use the EasyStep

Interview and the postinterview cleaning require the following items:

* Accurate financial statements as of the conversion-to-QuickBooks date

Full accounting of your accounts payables and accounts receivable as well as inventory and fixed assets

• A full or almost complete list of customers, employees vendors, other inventory elements (if you purchase or sell your inventory)

You'll need to put all of this information together before you begin with the EasyStep Interview because you're asked to answer these questions in the course of your interview. Don't rush around looking for specific pieces of information as you conduct the interview. Gather all the relevant information up front. After that, you can stack the required papers on your desk beside your computer.

Also, I'd like to point out that you'll have to make various accounting decisions while you complete this EasyStep Interview. You can, for instance, decide if you'd like to utilize an accounts payable program. You're asked by QuickBooks whether you'd like to provide customers with monthly statements. Also, QuickBooks asks you if you'd like to create estimates for your customers. You're also asked if you'd like to take classes to monitor your spending and income.

If you're confronted with one of the financial questions you are able to just choose the answer that comes up. But, you're obliged by law to maintain consistency in your accounting to meet tax reasons. If you'd like to change your accounting method -- which is known as a change in methods of accounting by Internal Revenue Service -- you'll need to request permission to change the method by the IRS.

One last note Make sure you keep the tax returns from the previous year on hand because it provides numerous details needed for your EasyStep Interview. For instance, the the tax return from last year provides the taxpayer identification number as well as the legal company name, as well as your way of accounting.

While you go through an interview you will work in QuickBooks to create the QuickBooks preferences (which will determine the manner in which QuickBooks operates and what features will be available) and then to set up your chart of accounts as well as banks accounts.

A chart of account to make it clear it is a way to identify the accounts for income, expense, asset, equity, and liability accounts that are shown on your financial statements.

When you've completed after you've completed the EasyStep Interview, you're almost prepared to get started with QuickBooks. In fact, in the case of a need it's possible to (after your EasyStep Interview) limp along using QuickBooks.

An important aspect to note A crucial point of clarification: You may think that you are prepared to rock and roll once you have installed QuickBooks and going through the EasyStep Interview. There are two QuickBooks setup tasks to finish following you have completed the EasyStep Interview: identify your starting trial balance , and then load your master key. The trial balance is a way to identify your year-to-date income and expenses numbers as well as your asset, liability and equity of the owner at the time of conversion. The master files contain the information you use frequently regarding vendors, customers employees, employees, as well as inventory items. For instance, the client master file holds a client's names and addresses, as well as their phone number, as well as the contact information for the person.

When you install the QuickBooks program The installation program will begin to start QuickBooks automatically, and then begin an EasyStep Interview. It is also possible to start with the EasyStep Interview by starting the QuickBooks program in the same manner as you open any other software.

The Welcome screen in the EasyStep Interview appears when you select to select the New Company command. The screen gives you general information on the process of setting up a new business within QuickBooks. The screen also contains hyperlinks, such as the one you use to contact an QuickBooks approved advisor. (QuickBooks advisors are, in fact are those who have completed the test for QuickBooks and have paid $500 to Intuit for an instance of QuickBooks and to be recognized on the QuickBooks website as an QuickBooks consultant.) You're likely to want to read the entire screen and then, when you're ready to start, select the button to start your interview.

This EasyStep Interview walks you through many screens of details. To go onto the next page, press Next. To return towards the prior screen select the Previous button. If you're down and feel discouraged and would like to quit then you can hit the leave button. However, try not to become discouraged.

Information about the company that is supplied

The initial few pages of your EasyStep Interview collect several important elements of general information regarding your company, such as the name of your company and the legal name of your company and address. You can also provide you federal tax ID and the month that you begin your fiscal year (typically January) The type of tax form your company uses to report to the IRS and the type of kind of business that you operate (retail services, retail, and so on).

After obtaining this general company details, QuickBooks creates the company data file, which contains the financial details of your business. QuickBooks offers the default name or QuickBooks data file that is based on the name of the company. All you have to accept is the suggested name as well as the suggested location of the folder.

Customizing QuickBooks

After QuickBooks takes in the general business details mentioned in the preceding paragraphs The EasyStep Interview asks you some specific questions about the way you manage your company, so that it can determine your QuickBooks preferences. The preferences, in essence, switch on or off different accounting features in QuickBooks and control the way QuickBooks functions and looks. Here are some examples of questions you will be asked during the EasyStep Interview asks to set the QuickBooks preferences:

* Does your firm maintain inventory?

Do you wish to keep track of the inventory you purchase and then sell?

* Do you take sales tax from your customers?

* When are you able to offer items for sale?

What format for invoice you would like to use to bill your customers?

Do you wish to utilize sales orders to monitor the backorders of customers and orders?

* Would you like to utilize QuickBooks to assist in the process of payroll for your employees?

* Do you need to write or create oral estimates for your clients?

* Do you prepare multiple invoices to provide an estimate (if you plan to use advance billing or partial billing)?

Do you want to keep track of the hours your employees or you spend on projects or jobs for your customers?

* Would you like to utilize classes to further separate expenses and income as well as liabilities, assets and equity owner's data?

• How would you wish to manage payments and bills (enter the checks directly, or simply enter the bills first, and then pay later)?

• How frequently do need to check Your Reminder List?

* Would you prefer to review reports on an annual rather than a cash base?

Setting your start date

One of the most crucial decisions you make when the process of setting up an account system would be to choose the date when you start using the new system. This is known as the date of conversion. It is generally recommended to begin using an accounting software at the beginning of the year, or on one of these dates: the day that marks the beginning of the calendar year, or on the first day of the month. In this regard, another important issue that the interviewer asks concerns the date of conversion. The interviewer will ask you to select the date when you first enter an interface. The most convenient time to begin with a new accounting system is in the beginning each year. The reason? You can make a more simple trial balance. When you begin the year, for instance you only enter balances for liability, asset and equity account of the owner. balances.

In addition, at any time, you can also input year-to-date expenses and income balances. Most of the time, this year-to date expenses and income information only at the beginning of each month. This is why the only alternative date to start your month that you could select is the beginning of the month.

In this scenario you will receive year-to-date earnings amounts until the closing of the previous month, based on your prior accounting system. If, for instance, you've used Peachtree and have year-to date expenses and income amounts from Peachtree.

Once you've provided the date of your start You've successfully completed the three steps of the interview. You've provided the essential company information, you've identified the bulk aspects of the accounting requirements you have and you've determined the date when you'd like to begin using QuickBooks. You're almost done.

The addition of accounts to banks

In your EasyStep interview, you'll be asked about the bank accounts you're using for your business. It's easy to mention the bank accounts. Then, you give your starting balance on the date of conversion.

Examining the chart suggested by accounts

Then, at the end in the EasyStep Interview, based on the details you provide regarding your business and the tax return forms you submit to IRS IRS, QuickBooks suggests a beginning set of accountsaccountants refer to it as chart of accounts. These are the categories used to keep track of your expenses, income as well as assets and equity of the owner. Accounts that QuickBooks checks by checking and the screen says which accounts are recommended. If you don't perform anything else, the checked accounts will be the ones you'll use (at minimum, at least for the initial time) in QuickBooks. But, you can also delete a suggested account through the click mark. QuickBooks eliminates the check mark, which means that the account will not figure in an account's final list of charts. It is also possible to click on an account to make an additional check mark, and then have it included in the beginning charts of account.

You can click on the Restore Recommendations link at the lower left of the page for a return to the initial chart of accounts that you were recommended to use (if you have made any changes that which you later decide that you don't would).

If the suggested chart of accounts seems acceptable to you, then click Next. You can accept the suggestions that QuickBooks suggests, since you will be able to alter the chart later on. accounts.

Viewing the QuickBooks Learning Center window

After you've completed your EasyStep Interview, QuickBooks displays the QuickBooks Learning Center window. The Learning Center window has clickable hyperlinks which you can click to access tutorials that give you a an "big picture" description of how to utilize QuickBooks. There's a lot of useful information there, so if you're new to QuickBooks take a look and look around. When you're done poking around through the site, press"Begin Using QuickBooks" or click the "Begin Using QuickBooks" button and the QuickBooks program window will open to full view. After that you are able entering accounting information in QuickBooks.

Start your EasyStep Interview and load the master file list. The master list of master files stores details that you can utilize and reuse. For instance the master file's lists lists every customer you have. The master file of information about your customers includes the name of the customer, address, contact details accounts numbers, and so on.

In this chapter, we'll guide you through the process of the process of adding information to each master file or lists like QuickBooks calls them that you'll need to complete (or generally complete) prior to using QuickBooks every day.

Important note Do not need to fill up all of your master files prior to begin to do anything.

If you add your current customers in the master file for customers as well as your current suppliers into your vendor master files and so on this amount of data could be enough to start. After entering the information during the EasyStep Interview and the addition of a few additional entries to key master data files, you might be able to include all the other information at a moment's notice. QuickBooks lets you include entries into the various master files while you navigate through dialog boxes and windows that refer to master file information.

Making the chart of Accounts List

It is the Chart of Accounts List is an account list that can be used to categorize earnings, expenses and liabilities, assets, and owner's equity amount. If you wish to see an individual element of the financial information in a report, you have to create an account to cover the line item. If you plan to budget using a specific line item, you will need an account to cover that budget amount. If you plan to include specific financial information in your taxes, then you'll require an account to gather particular information.

Fortunately, the steps to making new accounts are easy. To create a brand new account on the Chart of Accounts List, follow these steps:

1. Select your ListsChart of Accounts command. QuickBooks shows its Chart of Accounts window.

2. Click on the Account button at in the lower right corner of the screen. QuickBooks opens an Account menu. One of the menu choices is New This is the command you can use to create an account.

3. Create a new account by selecting the New option on the account menu. QuickBooks will display its first Add Account window. Account window.

4. Make use of the buttons for Type to determine which type of account you're adding. QuickBooks offers the following types of accounts such as: Income, Expense Fixed Assets Credit Card, Loan

Equity as well, when you select"Other Accounts" Type and then open another account in the Other Accounts Type drop-down menu Accounts Receivable Other Current Asset Other Assets, Accounts Payable Others Current Liability Long-Term Liability the cost for goods that are sold Other income, and other expenses. These groups of accounts inform QuickBooks the area in which the financial statement that information is recorded. It is important to note that the initial Add new Account window displays examples of the chosen account type. It is located over both the Continue and Cancel button commands.

5. Click Continue. QuickBooks opens another Add New Account dialog.

6. You can use the Name box provide your new account with an unique name. The name you choose for the account will be displayed in your bank statements.

7. When the new account one that is a subaccount that is the parent account, then determine the parent account using the Subaccount Of checkbox. When you've clicked the checkbox for Subaccount Of identify the parent account selecting the Subaccount Of drop-down list.

8. Other account details are required. In addition, the Add New Account will include an Bank Acct. No. box to note the account number for a specific bank account. Other types of accounts may contain similar boxes for the storage of details about the account. For instance the credit card version of the Add Account window. Account window allows you to save information about the number of your credit card. If you have a box or two you can store your account details you can make use of it, if needed to gather the bits and pieces of information you'd like to keep.

9. Choose the tax line the tax line that the account data will be disclosed by selecting the tax form and the tax line in the Tax-Line Mapping drop-down list. There's no need to add a specific account to an tax line if information isn't included on the tax return of your business. For instance the balances of cash accounts aren't included on the tax return of a sole proprietor. Therefore, a bank account of sole proprietors does not contain any tax line information. Cash balances are reported in the tax returns for a corporate entity however. Therefore, if you're adding bank account to a company using to use the Tax-Line Mapping drop-down list to identify the tax line which bank account data is recorded.

126

Once you have described the new account you'd like to establish You can then select OK to save your brand new account on the Chart of Accounts List. It is also possible to hit Next to save the account's information and then display your Add New Account screen so you can add another account.

This is basically everything you have to learn about creating accounts. One other point to mention is the fact that Account MenuThis is the menu of options that QuickBooks displays when you hit the Account button in the Chart of Accounts window -it also offers a number of useful commands to work with accounts. The menu offers a delete command to erase the selected account (as as you haven't previously used that account). The menu offers an Edit button which you can click to modify the account details you have selected. The Account menu offers additional commands that you could utilize to manipulate this Chart of Accounts List. The majority of them are self-descriptive names for commands: Print List, Create Inactive and others.

The button for Activities located at the lower right in the Chart of Accounts window, provides a menu of commands you can use to make checks, deposit checks or enter credit card charges or transfer funds, enter journal entries and reconcile bank accounts and also use a register. The Reports button will display a menu of commands you can utilize to print reports with details about your account.

The Item List is set up

If you select the ListsItem List option, QuickBooks displays the Item List window. Its Item List window lists all the items you've setup in the course of conducting an EasyStep Interview and items that you've manually added after conducting your EasyStep Interview. It is possible to add additional items into the list by following the instructions on screen within Quickbooks.

Work with working with Price Level List

The Price Level List lets you create price adjustments that you could make on the fly when you invoice your customers, issue credit memos, and so on. Since this Price Level List directly relates to how you handle and invoice to inventory item.

Using Sales Tax Codes

Its Sales Tax Codes List keeps an inventory of codes, or abbreviations that are used to identify things as tax-deductible or not. If you select this option, QuickBooks displays a window that lists the available code for sales taxes. (Usually there are two codes in the list that are Tax and Non.)

To create a new sale tax number, just click on the Sales Tax Code button, select New and then write a description of your new tax. It's important to note that the Sales Tax Code List doesn't show up unless you instruct QuickBooks to keep track of sales tax.

The process of setting up a payroll item List

The Payroll Item List lists things that are listed on employee pay stubs for their payroll. When you're using an external payroll service provider to handle all of your pay -- which is not a bad thingyou don't have to think regarding paying attention to the payroll Item List. If you're using QuickBooks's assisted Payroll Service Don't be concerned regarding paying attention to the payroll Item List. In the case of QuickBooks Premier Payroll Service, you don't need to worry about it. QuickBooks Premier Payroll Service, it's not necessary to keep track of payroll in

QuickBooks since the QuickBooks users do it from their office on their personal computers.

If you are required to add items to your payroll Follow these steps:

1. Select from the list of Payroll Item List option. QuickBooks opens its Payroll Item List window.

2. To add a new payroll Item Click on the Payroll Item button and then select New in the Payroll Item menu. QuickBooks will display an Add New Payroll Item dialog box. It is possible to set up a new item for payroll or use the EZ Set-Up method or Custom Set Up Method. If you'd like QuickBooks to aid you in creating a standard payroll item Click to the EZ Set Up button, then click Next, and follow the instructions on screen. If you'd like to create an individual setup for an item for payroll you can select the Custom Set Up button, and then click proceed to the next. QuickBooks will guide you through a multi-screen interview such as that of the EasyStep Interview that asks you about the type of payroll item you wish to create. For instance, the first dialog box QuickBooks will display asks you to choose the kind of payroll item you would like to create. Answer this question by choosing any of the options after that, clicking Next.

3. Name the item on your payroll. Once you've identified the kind of item that you pay for, you identify it. QuickBooks offers a different variant of the Add New Payroll Item dialog box . It has a field that you can must fill in for the item to be given a title.

4. For the final step of the setup of your payroll item then click Next to proceed through the remaining questions regarding the setup of your payroll item. You will be able to identify that the agency that you are paying the debt as well as the taxpayer identification code that uniquely identify your taxing organization and the account for liability that you use to track items as well as that tax line you utilize to report the expense as well as the rules QuickBooks must follow to calculate the amount (such as whether or not the item is tax-exempt) as well as a handful of other bits of information.

Once you have filled in all the details and then hit"Finish" (which is on the latest edition of the Add New Payroll Item dialog box), QuickBooks adds the new payroll item to the Payroll Item List. Payroll Item menu Payroll Item menu supplies commands that can be used to work using this Payroll Item List.

The process of creating a customer list

A Customer List helps keep the track of all your customers as well as your customer's details. For instance the Customer List tracks billing addresses and shipping addresses of customers.

These steps will allow you to include customers in the customer list:

1. Select your CustomersCustomer Center command. QuickBooks will display an Customer Center window.

2. To add a new client Click the New Customer and Job button, and then select the New Customer option. QuickBooks shows an New Customer screen.

3. Use the Customer Name field to give your customer the name of a shorter version. You don't have to type the full name of the customer in the customer name box. This information can be entered in the Company Name box shown on the Address Info tab. You'll need an abbreviated version of the customer's name that you could use to reference the customer in QuickBooks. QuickBooks software for accounting.

4. (Usual Standard) (Usual Rule): Don't bother with opening balance and as of boxes. It is not recommended to establish the customer's initial balance with both the opening Balance as well as As of boxes. It's not the correct method of setting the new receivables of your customer account balance. If you follow this method you're basically setting up the debit component of an entry but without the credit component.

5. Utilize the boxes in the Address Info tab to enter the name of your company, along with the contact details as well as shipping and billing addresses, contact names telephone number, contact number, the number for fax and so on.

6. Give a few more information about the customer. When you click on the Additional Information Tab, QuickBooks displays several other boxes you can use to store and collect information about customers. For instance, you can make use of the Type drop-down list to identify a person according to a specific "customer category." Utilize the Terms drop-down menu to determine the default terms of payment for the customer. Utilize the Rep drop-down list for identifying the sales rep of the customer's default. Then, select your Preferred

Method of Send Method to choose the method that is used to send the invoices of the customer and credit memos. You can also add the resale number, choose the default price, and select on the Define Fields button to specify additional fields that you would like to gather and report to the customer.

7. Click on the payment Info tab to open the list of boxes. You can enter the account number of the customer and credit limit, as well as the preferred method of payment.

The Setting Up of the Vendor List

Similar to how you utilize a Customer List for keeping records of all your clients, you also use the Vendor List to maintain the records of your vendors. Similar to the Customer List, the Vendor List allows you to collect and keep track of information like the address of the vendor as well as the contact number and more.

To add a vendor your Vendor List Follow these steps:

1. Select your VendorsVendor Center command. If you do this, QuickBooks displays the Vendor Center window.

2. To create a new vendor, select the Add Vendor button. QuickBooks opens an New Vendor window.

3. Give the vendor an initial name within the Vendor Name field. Like the Customer Job list, can use this name to identify the vendor in QuickBooks. Therefore, an abbreviation works. It's all about having something simple to type in and simple to remember.

4. (Usual Rule) (Usual Rule): Don't look at opening balance and as of fields. Don't use opening balance and as of boxes. The uninitiated utilize these boxes to write down the balance due to an opening vendor, and the date on which the balance is due. However, this can cause issues later. In the near future, that miserable accountant of the soul will have to discover and rectify this mistake. In the case of adding new customers, there is some exceptions to the standard rule is in place, as explained in the next tip.

The general rule is to not have to set an open balance on vendors, this rule is not without exception. It is important to record your balance in your accounts payable at the time of conversion when you set an opening balance on each vendor on the date of conversion. The total of these opening balances is the one QuickBooks utilizes to calculate your total account payable on the date of conversion.

5. Provide the address of the vendor. In the Address Info tab, you can enter information about your vendor's address. Address Info tab provides an array of boxes that are easy to understand which you can use to gather names of vendors and information about their addresses. It is recommended that you enter the full name of the vendor into the box for Company Name. Then, click on the Address Details button and open another dialog box , dubbed"Edit Address Information" Edit Address Information dialog box where you can enter the address in the typical street address city, state, and ZIP code formats.

6. Provide any additional information you think is necessary. When you click on the Additional Information Tab, QuickBooks displays a handful of additional boxes that can be used to gather and record information, like your account number, that vendor's number, your type of vendor as well as the payment terms you are using to pay the vendor as well as your credit limit and the tax ID number of the vendor. Tax ID numbers are vital if

you are later required to give this vendor an official 1099 form in order to report the amount of money you paid him.

An excellent guideline to follow when paying an individual vendor for the first time is to ask for the tax identification number of his. If a person isn't willing to provide you with his tax ID numberwhich makes it impossible to declare the money you pay them -- then it's an indication that something is that's not quite right.

Set up an Asset List for Fixed Assets

If you select to use the ListsFixed Asset Item List option, QuickBooks displays the Fixed Asset Item List window. This window allows you to view the list of fixed items -- furnishings, machines, machines vehicles, and so on that you've purchased. You can, at the minimum, once you've clicked an Item button, select New on the left menu and fill out your information in the New Item window for each fixed asset.

The Fixed Asset List doesn't really work with it's QuickBooks general ledger. It is used to record the purchase or removal of fixed assets with the standard QuickBooks transactions. You could, for instance, document buying a certain fixed asset by simply writing checks in the normal way. You could also document the disposal of fixed assets making an entry in the general ledger journal.

The Fixed Assets List is then serves as a separate list that helps you keep an eye on the fixed assets you bought. Because it's independent, I'm not planning to talk much about the list in any of the volumes in this resource. I'll also mention that your CPA likely -- but not certainly -- has an inventory that lists your assets fixed, as she requires this list to accurately include depreciation in your tax return and on your accounting statements (if you have CPA assistance in preparing these). This is why some people -- like me , see the list of fixed asset items as somewhat redundant.

9: Acounting

The discussion of how you can make use of QuickBooks to manage your business starts by introducing the fundamentals of accounting. This chapter will provide the same information you will get in a college-level accounting class. The entire chapter is designed to be tailored to QuickBooks and the small-business setting. The information you'll find this and the subsequent chapters in this book is a good overview of the accounting process in a small-sized business setting with QuickBooks.

If you've worked in accounting, and are familiar with reading the income statement and balance sheet, or know how to write an entry in a journal then you don't need to read this chapter.

If you're new to the world of accounting and bookkeeping, you should take the time to read the chapter carefully. The chapter begins by providing an description of the goal of accounting. We then review the standard financial statements that every accounting system of any kind creates. We also go over some of the fundamental principles of accounting and the philosophies of accounting. In the final part, we discuss little about the law of income tax as well as tax accounting.

The purpose of Accounting

At its core accounting is a perfect rational sense. The larger picture "The most crucial aspect" to know concerning accounting is it gives financial information to STAKEHOLDERS.

Stakeholders are people who conduct business with or are in contact with a company which includes managers as well as employees, investors vendors, banks as well as government officials and organizations that can tax a company. Stakeholders and the information they require need to be discussed more. Why? Because the needs of these parties determine what an accounting system should do.

Investors, managers entrepreneurs, investors, and managers

The first group of stakeholders comprises the company's managers as well as investors and entrepreneurs. The latter group requires financial information to determine if a business is earning money. They also require information that will reveal the extent to which a company is growing or shrinking, and the state of health or illness it is. To meet its obligations and responsibilities, this group frequently requires detailed data. For instance, a supervisor or entrepreneur might need to be aware of which customers are most profitable, or even unprofitable. A savvy investor might be interested in knowing what product lines are expanding or shrinking.

A similar set of information requirements relates to recording of liabilities and assets. A asset is anything the company owns for example, cash, inventory or other equipment. A liability is a obligation or debt the company owes for example, the loans of banks and accounts payable.

Naturally, someone in an organization -- possibly an administrator, bookkeeper or accountant must have precise documents of the amount of money the company has in its banks, the inventory that the company keeps in its storage facility and on shelves and the equipment the company owns and utilizes to conduct its business.

When you go through the previous paragraphs, nothing you read is particularly shocking. It's all logical, isn't it? Anybody who works in a company, runs the business, or invests in a company requires accurate and general information on the financial operations of the company and, in many instances highly detailed information regarding the most important financial assets (such in the cash) or the liabilities (such such as loans from banks).

External lenders, Banks

A different group of stakeholders comprises external companies that lend money to businesses and credit reporting agencies that provide details to the lenders. For instance, banks would like to be aware of the financial and financial situation of a company prior to making loans. The accounting system must generate the financial information banks require in order to approve the loan request.

Examining the REVIEW OF THE COMMON FINANCIAL Statements

After the background information presented, let's look at some of the more common accounting statements or financial statements that an accounting system such as QuickBooks produces. If you know what reports you would like the accounting software to create It will be simpler to gather the necessary raw data for the preparation of these reports.

In the sections that follow the three most important financial statements are reviewed The income statement, the balance sheetand report of flows. Also, briefly discussed is the fourth category, which is a catch-all of financial reports.

It is important to know what accounts your systems for accounting are required to prepare and what data the financial statements provide.

The Income Statement

The most important financial report that an accounting system generates includes the statement of income. The income statement can also be often referred to as an income statement or a loss and profit statement. A statement of income summarizes the company's revenue and expenses over a specific time. Revenues refer to the money businesses earn by offering products and services to customers. The expenses represent the amount the company spends on providing these products and services. If a company is able to provide products or services to its customers in order to earn more than expenses, it is able to earn profits. If the expenses are greater than revenues then, naturally, the business has to pay a loss.

To demonstrate how this worksand it's quite easy to understand, check out the following tables. Table 1-1 summarizes the revenue that an imaginary company makes. Table 2 lists the expenses that the business has to incur over the same time. The two tables give the necessary information to create an income report.

Table 1-1

A Sales Journal

Joe $1,000

Bob 500

Frank 1,000

Abul 2,000

Yoshio 2,750

Marie 2,250

Jeremy 1,000

Chang 2,500

Total sales $13,000

Table 1 and 2 An Expenses Journal

Purchases of buns and dogs $3,000.

Rent 1,000

Earnings of Earnings of 4,000

1,000 supplies

Total supplies of $9,000

With the data from these tables, it is possible to create an income statement that is simple as illustrated by the below table. Understanding the essentials of the income statement is crucial to understanding the way accounting functions and what accounting attempts to accomplish. So, I'd like to provide some depth about the income statement.

Table 3 Simple Income Statement

Sales revenue $13,000

The cost of goods sold at 3,000

Gross margin of $10,000

Operating costs

Rent $1,000

Pays Earnings of 4,000

Supplies 1,000

Total operating expenses of 6,000

Operating Profit $4,000

One of the first things to take note of in the income statement in Table 1 is the income figure, which was $13,000. This figure represents the revenue generated for an exact period of time. The figure of $13,000 in Table 1-3 is derived straight from the Sales Journal shown in Table 1-1.

The most important thing to remember when it comes to accounting for sales revenues is that sales revenue is recorded when services or goods are offered, not when the customer purchases the product or services. If you take a look at the list of sales in Table 1-1 for instance, Joe (the first customer that is listed) could have paid $1000 in cash, however Bob, Frank, and Abdul (the third, second as well as the fourth customer) could have made their purchases using credit card. Yoshio, Marie, and Jeremy (the fifth, sixth and seventh customers on the list) might not even made a purchase when the items or services were offered. They could have offered to pay for their purchases later. However, the time of purchase does not matter. Accounting professionals have discovered that revenue is counted when the goods or services are offered. Information about the time when the customers pay for those products or services, should you require this information, could be gleaned from customer payment lists.

Balance sheet

The second and most significant financial statement an accounting system generates is the balance sheet. A balance sheet is a report of the company's assets, liabilities as well as the owner's contributions to capital at a certain date.

The assets that appear on the balance sheet are belonging to the business, are of value and that were paid for with money.

* The liability figures on the balance sheet are amount that a company owes to other businesses, individuals as well as government agencies.

* The contributions of the owner's capital are the sums that owners, partners or shareholders have

147

deposited into the company through investments or have invested in the business through leaving the profits within the business.

If you are able to comprehend the definition of assets and liabilities the basis of a balance sheet, it is simple to comprehend and understand. Table 1-4, for instance illustrates a basic balance sheet. Imagine that this balance sheet reveals the state of the stand prior to the start each day but before any hot dogs were sold. The first section of your balance sheet reveals what are the assets and liabilities of your business of a hot dog stand including the cash deposit of $1,000 into the cash register that is placed in an under counter box and the $3000 worth of buns and hot dogs that you've bought to sell throughout the day.

Table 1 - A Basic Balance Sheet

Assets

Cash $1,000

Inventory of 3,000

Total assets of $4,000

Liability

Accounts payable of $2,000

The loan is payable in the amount of $1,000

Equity in the Owner

S. Nelson, capital 1,000

Total liabilities and equity of owner $4,000

The balance sheets can utilize a number of different categories for reporting assets like the accounts payable (these are the amounts that customers have to pay) as well as fixtures, investments, equipment and long-term investment. For small-sized owner-operated businesses there are a few of the asset categories are listed. If you take a look at your balance sheets of large company -- for instance among the top 100 biggest companies across the United States -- you will see these additional categories.

The liability section on the balance sheet lists the amount the company is owed by other individuals and companies. For instance the balance sheet in Table 1-4 displays the amount of accounts payable at $2,000 as well as an amount of loan due in the amount of $1,000. Most likely, the $2,000 in accounts payable represents the amount due to vendors who supplied hot buns and dogs. The loan amount of $1,000 is the amount you've borrowed maybe from a innocent and wise friend.

The section on equity for the owner's indicates the amount the owner, shareholders, or partners are contributing to the company by way of initial capital or dividends reinvested. An important aspect to note about the balance sheet as shown in Table 1-4is that this balance sheet reveals how the owner's equity appears when the business operates as a sole proprietorship. If you are sole proprietors there is only one line listed in the equity section of the owner on the balance sheet. The line includes every contribution made by owner including amounts initially invested as well as those that are that are reinvested.

I'll make two key observations regarding the balance sheet in Table 1 - 4. A balance sheet has to have a balance. That signifies that all assets should be equal to the total liabilities as well as equity of the owner. The balance sheet as shown in Table 1-4, as an example, total assets appear as $4,000. Total liabilities and equity of the owner are also shown as $4,000. This isn't a accident. If an accounting system functions well and the accountants as well as bookkeepers who input information into the system follow the correct procedures The balance sheet should be balanced.

A balance sheet is an overview of the company's financial position at a certain date. For instance, I say in the opening remarks to Table 4 that the balance sheet in this table reveals the financial status for the stand's hot dogs prior to the start of the day's business operations.

It is possible to prepare the balance sheet for any time. It is essential to understand the fact that a balance sheet was created for a specific point in time.

According to the convention, businesses create balance sheets in order to display the financial situation in the final span of time during which an income statement is written. For instance, a company usually prepares an income statement every year. In this case it is also necessary to create an account of balance at the close in the course of the calendar year.

Table 1-5 illustrates how the equity section of an owner on a balance sheet will look for the partnership. On Table 1-5 I illustrate how the equity section of the owner of the business of a hot dog stand appears when instead of having an owner who is solely named S. Nelson running the hot dog stand, it is actually operated and owned by three partners with the names of Tom, Dick, and Harry. In this scenario the equity of the partners section displays the initial amounts invested as well as any funds that were that are reinvested through the partnership. Like with sole proprietorships, all of the partners' contributions and reinvested profits are shown on one line.

Table 1-5 Equity of the Owner in Partnerships

Equity of Partners

Tom Capital $500

Dick capital 250

Harry Capital 250

Capital of the total partner: $1000

Have an examination of Table 1 -. It outlines the way the equity section for the owner is viewed by a company.

Table 1-1 Owner's Equity of a Corporation

Equity of shareholders

Capital stock 100 shares for $1 per $100

Contributed capital greater than par 400

Retained earnings of 500

Equity of the total shareholder is $1,000

The following part is a bit odd. In the case of a corporation the numbers that appear within the shareholder's equity section or shareholder's equity segment can be classified into two primary categories which are: retained earnings and capital contributed. Retained earnings refer to profits that shareholders have left the company. Contributed capital is money that was initially donated by shareholders to the company.

The concept of retained earnings is logical, doesn't it? It's the money - -that is, the profits that investors have invested into the company.

The concept of contributed capital is more complex. This is the way it works: If you purchase a share stock in a brand new corporation -- say, $5 , generally, a portion of that price per share will be for par value. Do not ask me to justify the par value. It's really a result of traditional business practices that were prevalent around a century ago or so. It is a good idea to be aware that generally in the event that you pay an amount, say , $5 for a share, a portion of what you pay, perhaps 10 cents per share, or $1 per shareis the par value.

In the owner's equity portion of a balance sheet, capital invested by investors who were the first to contribute is broken down into amount paid for this mystery par value as well as the amount that are paid over the par value. For instance, in Table 1-6, it is possible to observe that the $100 in shareholder's equity or owner's Equity is the amount paid in par value. A further $400 of the money that were contributed by the investors who originally made the investment represent amounts paid over the par value. Equity of the total shareholder or total shareholder's equity, is equal to the total of the capital par value of stock as well as the capital contribution and the excess from par value as well as any earnings that are retained. In Table 1-6, the total equity of shareholders is $1,000.

Statement of cash flow

Here's the only financial statement that is difficult one that is the cash flows.

Before I start I've got one point to make regarding the statement of flows in cash. Whatever handholding and explanations accountants give certain people are unable to understand the numbers on the statements of cash flows. Actually, a lot students majoring in accounting do not (in my view at a minimum) really understand the way a cash flow statement flows really functions.

Therefore, don't be too busy looking at this statement , or trying to comprehend the significance of it. QuickBooks provides a report of cash flow, however you don't have to make use of this type of statement. In reality, QuickBooks produces cash basis income statements that give you similar details, and in a much more readable format.

I believe the most effective method to explain the purpose of the statement of cash flows accomplishes is to to take a look at the balance sheet that was shown earlier in Table 4. It represents the cash flow balance of the hot dog stand that was imagined at the start in the morning.

Take a look at Table 1-7. It shows what the balance sheet looks like at close of the day, when operations at the stand for hot dogs are completed. You will notice that at the beginning in the morning, money was equal to $1,000. By the close of the day, cash is equal to $5,000. The cash flow statement clarifies why cash fluctuates from one to the other number over time. In the same way, a statement of cash flow explains the process of how money changes from $1,000 at the beginning of the day and reaches $5,000 at the close in the course of the day.

Table 1-7 A Simple Balance Sheet

Assets

Cash $5,000

Inventory Zero

Total assets of $5,000

Liability

Accounts to be paid $0

The loan is due in the amount of at the rate of 0

Equity of the owner

S. Nelson, capital S. Nelson, capital

Total liabilities and equity of owner $5,000

Table 1-8, which is not a coincidence is a chart of cash flow that describes the flow of cash to your hypothetical hot dog stand. In the event that you're reading this article, most likely, you'll need to comprehend this particular statement. I begin with the lowest point of the sentence and move towards the top.

Table 1-8 An Easy Statement of Cash Flows

Operation activities

Net income $4,000

Reduce in the amount of accounts payable (2,000)

Adjustment of inventory

Net cash generated through operating activities of $5,000

Activities of financing

Notes payable to be reduced (1,000)

Net cash received (used) in finance activities (1,000)

Increase in cash to 4,000

Cash balance at the start of the period 1000

Cash balance at the end of period is $5,000

In the tradition of accountants, they show negative numbers in parentheses. These parentheses are more clear in indicating negative numbers as a simple minus symbol could.

The three lines that make up an accounting statement for cash flows are easy to comprehend. The cash balance at end of the time period, $5,000 represents the amount of cash the company has at the time of its closing. The balance at the beginning of the day, $1000 represents the cash the business has at the start in the morning. The total cash position at beginning of the period, and the balance at the end of the period are tied to the cash balances shown on the two balance sheets. (Look at Table 1-7 and Table 1-4 to verify this claim.) It is clear that if you begin the period with $1,000 , and end it with $5,000, the cash value will have increased to $4,000. It's a mathematical certainty. There's no question, isn't there?

The financing activities on the cash flow statement flows illustrate how borrowing from firms and debt repayment affects the firm's cash flow. If the business that operates a hot dog stand makes use of its profits to pay back the loan of $1,000 - in this particular instance, this is exactly what happened the cash outflow of $1,000 shows in the financing part of the cash statement flows as negative $1,000.

The top part of the cash flow statement flows can be the most difficult to grasp. Be aware, however, that I've covered the rest of the statement. Therefore, with a firm effort, you'll be able to fight your way to understand what's happening here.

The operating activities section of the cash statement flows basically shows the cash generated from the profits. When you examine Table 1-8 for instance you will find that the top line of the operating activity section in the report of cash flow is the net profit of $4000. It's the net profit amount shown in the statement of income for that period. However, the net profit or operating profit that is reported on the income statement of the company isn't always the same as cash income or profit. Many factors need to be adjusted to transform this net income amount into what's basically an operating profit in cash.

In the instance of the hot dog stand business, if , for instance, you make use of some of the profit to cover all accounts payable, the payoff takes up a portion of your cash profits. The table 1-8 demonstrates. It is evident that the drop in accounts payable amount from $2,000 to 0 during the day was very logically that you pay $2,000 of your net profit. Another way of thinking about this is that you used the cash profit of $2,000 to pay back accounts payable. Keep in mind that the account payable is the amount you owe your vendors for buns and hot dogs.

Another adjustment is needed to account for the reduction in inventory. The decline in inventory that occurs from the beginning of the period through the conclusion of the time period results in cash. It's basically a matter of liquidating the inventory. Another way to look at this is that, even though the inventory -- like buns and hot dogs in our case is listed as an expense on the income statement for the day however, it wasn't bought at the time of purchase. It's not a cash-based item in the course of the day, but it was bought in the past.

When you add the net income as well as the adjustment to the accounts payable and the adjustment to inventory to receive the net cash provided by operating activities. The table 1-8 shows that these three numbers add up to $5,000 in cash generated by operations.

When you are familiar with the specifics of the operating and financing activities sections of the statement flow of cash report is logical. The net cash generated by operating activities amounts to $5,000. Financing activities cut the cash amount by $1,000. That means that cash actually increased during the period by $4,000 which is why the cash amount starts at $1,000, and closes the time at $5,000.

Other statements of accounting

You could think of some examples of other useful or popular accounting reports. Unsurprisingly, a great accounting software like QuickBooks can produce the majority such reports. For instance, one popular report known as a financial statement, is listing of the sums your customers owe to you. It's recommended to review and prepare these reports regularly to ensure that your customers don't end up who are causing collection issues.

Table 1-9 illustrates how the simple type of report on accounts receivables could appear: Every customer is identified along with the amount they owe.

Table 1-9 A Report on Accounts Receivable at the End of the Day

Customer	Amount
W. Churchill	$45.12
G. Patton	34.32
B. Montgomery	12.34
H. Petain	65.87
C. de Gaulle	43.21
Total receivables	$200.86

Table 1-10 illustrates another typical accounting report, an inventory report that a hot dog stand might be able to provide at the beginning in the morning. A report on inventory similar to that in Table 1-10 will likely identify the different items that are available for resale, their quantity that is in stock, and the price (or value) of inventory items. An inventory report like this can be useful in ensuring that you have the right amount of inventory available. (Think of how helpful this kind of report would be if you planned to sell thousands of hot dogs during major sports events in your city.)

Table 1-10 A Report on Inventory at the Start of Day

Quantity of the item

Kielbasa 2000 $900.00

Bratwurst 2000 1,000.00

Simple buns, 2000 500.00

Singame Buns 2000 600.00

Total inventory $3,000.00

Connecting it all up Now, you'll know the function of an accounting system. If you reduce everything to its core it's easy isn't it? In reality, an accounting system is merely a way to provide users with financial data needed to manage your company.

Let me make a side-by-side but crucial idea. QuickBooks provides all of these accounting details. The majority of the time creating these types of financial statements with QuickBooks is surprisingly simple. However, before you can do that, you'll find it beneficial to understand something about bookkeeping and accounting. Be aware that the broad picture that is covered within this chapter are the most crucial information you'll need. If you can grasp the concepts that are discussed in this chapter, the fight is greater than half over.

Chapter 10: Bookkeeping

Customers who are invoiced

QuickBooks has a number of tools to assist you in billing your customers. I'll outline these tools along with several other tools for recording payments to customers and for distributing credit memos.

If you've been billing customers manually using a manual process -- maybe you've created invoices using an application like Word processor -- you'll find QuickBooks an excellent help. In addition, QuickBooks help you with invoicing and other tasks more efficient however, it also records invoice data, and records the information into QuickBooks data files. QuickBooks information file. It is a good thing that you can also enjoy the benefit of simply recording accounting transactions through QuickBooks to invoice.

Invoice Forms: Choosing the Right One

QuickBooks lets you use an invoice form that is compatible with the needs of your business. For instance, companies who sell products require an invoice with details of the items that are offered for sale. Businesses that sell servicesfor instance, a law firm, or an architectural company -- require an invoice that adequately defines the services. Companies that sell both goods as well as services require a combination of features. It is good to know that QuickBooks permits you to select the best invoice format that is suited to your business.

For choosing an invoice format show your Create Invoices window, by selecting the CustomersCreate Invoices option. If QuickBooks opens it's Create Invoices Window, you can use the Template drop-down menu located in the upper-right corner of the window. This allows you to select the invoice type you'd like to use. The dropdown menu offers options like an attorney's bill as well as a finance charge invoicing or a fixed-fee invoice or product invoice, an invoice for service as well as professional invoices. Select the invoice template you think is going most appropriate for your company. QuickBooks changes its Create Invoices window whenever you select a new invoice template. This means that you will be able to check out what an invoice template appears like by selecting one in the Form Template drop-down list.

The ability to customize an invoice form

While you can select an invoice template that is pre-defined to create invoices, QuickBooks allows you to do more than the other options. You can also make your own invoice template to create an invoice that is exactly the way you prefer. To accomplish this begin with an invoice templates, and then alter it until it meets your specific needs.

Selecting a template that you can customize

To select a template you want to personalize, open the Create Invoices window. This can be done by selecting the CustomersCreate Invoices option. Then select on the Customize button. QuickBooks will display its Basic Customization dialogue box. You might need to expand your Create Invoices window to view the Customize button. To identify the invoice template you'd like to modify Click to the Manage Templates button, and then when QuickBooks opens the Manage Templates dialog box, select the invoice template you wish to modify. QuickBooks initially provides a customized invoice template as well as a finance charge template that you can modify.

You can also click on one of these templates and select Copy for the creation and modify one of these templates. If You click OK QuickBooks will close its Manage Templates dialog box and brings users in your Basic Customization dialog box.

Customization of invoices is easy.

This dialog box, called Basic Customization offers a variety of easy-to-create invoice customization options. When you customize these options -- and I will explain how to do this in the next paragraphs -you will notice that QuickBooks alters the Preview box on the right side in the Basic Customization dialog box so you can see how your modifications appear like. First, I will explain how you can make the modifications.

Logo

If you want to add a logo your invoices, click your Use Logo check box. When QuickBooks shows your Select Image dialog box (not visible) make use of it to choose the graphic image file which displays your logo. It is a Select Image dialog box works similar to a typical Windows open dialog box for file selection.

Colors

To include color on your invoices, say you own an inkjet printer with color and don't mind whether you pay a little amount of money on colored inkChoose the color scheme that you would like to apply in the Select Color Scheme drop-down list. After that, click on the Apply Color Scheme button.

Making a mess with invoice fonts

You can pick the font QuickBooks uses for the various bits of text included on invoices. Simply select the portion of text you'd like to change from the Font For box, then select on the change Font button. QuickBooks opens its Example Dialog box. You can use the Font Size, Font Style and size boxes define what the chosen bit of text should appear like. Its Example dialog box also includes the Sample box which illustrates how your font will change appearance. Once you've completed the specification of the font then click OK.

For identifying Company & Transaction information

Its Company & Transaction Information options will let you specify the details should be included on the template of the form. Choose the check box that corresponds to the piece of information you want to include. If you wish to have the company's name to be displayed on your invoiceit means that you're not using pre-printed invoice or letterhead forms, select the checkbox for Company Name.

If you want to alter certain aspects of your company's information Click on the button to update information. QuickBooks will then display you with the Company Information dialog box, that you can use to modify or change your company's names, addresses, phone number, and more.

Examining the additional customization options

If you are unable to create invoices that appear exactly how you would like them to by using the options that are available in the Basic Customization window the next step is to select the Additional Customization option. QuickBooks will open an Additional Customization dialogue box. This dialog box offers you greater control over the information you see on your invoices as well as the way invoices are printed. It isn't possible to utilize the Additional Customization option in the event that you're using one of the standard invoice templates, but only in the case of copies of the template. In this case, QuickBooks may prompt you to create a copy of the invoice template if you hit the Additional Customization button.

Invoicing a customer

In order to invoice a client to invoice a customer, you must use an invoice, use the Create Invoices window. This allows you to identify the customer and indicate the amount the customer is liable for. To open the Create Invoices window select the CustomersCreate Invoices option. Once you have done that, QuickBooks displays a Create Invoices window. In the past, we have mentioned that you are able to use different types for invoice forms. You may also opt to modify the invoice form so that it is in line with the requirements of your business. In the next steps I'll explain, generally the process of invoicing customers. The specific steps you follow could be slightly different if you're using an invoice form template with a different format.

Close your Open Window List by clicking the close box (the small box by an X in the upper-right corner this list). To display your Open Window List after you've closed it, click ViewOpen Window List. When you've displayed the Create Invoices window, you must follow the following steps to bill the customer:

Determine the customer's name and, if necessary identify the job. For this to be done, choose the customer, customer and job from the drop-down list Customer:Job. Do not worry regarding this "job" company if you aren't experienced with it. However, you must be aware of how customers operate. You need to identify the particular customer you're billing. This can be done by choosing the customer from the list of jobs in the Customer:Job. In the event that the user is a brand new customer to whom you haven't yet been invoiced or listed on the Customer List you must enter a concise name for the client -such as an abbreviation for the business name of the customerin the list of Jobs in the Customer. QuickBooks will then indicate that the customer doesn't appear in the Customer List and asks if you'd like to add that customer. You must make sure you say yes. When asked, you must provide the information about the customer that QuickBooks asks for. You can also categorize an invoice to fall to a particular category using the drop-down menu for classes. Do not be concerned about class tracking.

Invoice confirmation or new header details. Once you have identified the customer, QuickBooks fills out the Date Invoice, Date To, Bill To and, perhaps

Shipping To fields. There is no have to alter any of these fields. It is recommended to review the information contained on these forms to be sure it's correct. For instance, you won't normally invoice anyone unless you've already delivered the product or service is already in place. Therefore, you should ensure that the date you invoice is in line with the date of shipment or the delivery of service date. It is also possible to confirm, for instance that the ship To address is correct. 3. Make sure to confirm or supply the details of the invoice field. Invoices contain information in the field that details things like purchase order numbers as well as payment terms, ship date and the shipping method. It is important to ensure that the information QuickBooks provides in these fields boxes is accurate. If a client has given you an order number, for instance you can enter the purchase order number in the P.O. Number box. Confirm that the payment conditions that are listed in the box for Terms are accurate. Verify that the date displayed on the Ship field is accurate. These fields do not have to be filled in for every invoice, but it is important to provide any details that make it easier for the client to pay the invoice, link an invoice to their purchase records, and understand the time and date an item will be delivered.

Let us describe the products that are sold.

The columns area on your invoice appears depends the type of product you're selling items or services. The columns area of the service appears simpler since there's not much detail in describing the items you sell. In the column area it is important to define each item -- every product or service for which you bill an invoice. In order to do this, make a single row for every item. The item you wish to charge for is then put to row 1, which is the column space. Each item you input the quantity you want to purchase and the code of the item, and the cost or price. QuickBooks pulls a description of the item from the Item List and then inserts this information in the description column. QuickBooks will also determine the cost of this item through multiplying the amount by the rate or price. However, you can modify both the Description as well as Amount field. If you modify the amount field QuickBooks adjusts the amount in the Each field by divising the amount by amount. In order to add additional items on the invoice, add additional rows. Every item you wish to invoice for -- every item that is an additional charge on the invoiceis listed as a line in the column section. If you are planning to invoice a client for a specific item, one line from the columns section of the invoice is utilized to describe the product. If you wish to charge customers for shipping one line in the invoice section explains that freight cost. If you wish to charge customers for sales tax the first line or row of the column area will show the sales tax charged.

Discounts

Discounts are a difficult line item to put in an invoice. Imagine that you would like to give a customer an additional discount of 25 percent. To do this, you already are aware (or you should be able to think) that you've included the discount line item in your bill. But, even though QuickBooks has a discount item in it's Item List, a discount percentage is only applicable to the prior line item in the bill. This is why QuickBooks provides subtotal line items. Subtotal line item to add up everything that was previously shown in the bill. By subtotaling all of the items on the product, such as it is possible for the company to offer the client the benefit of a discount of 25% on these items. You must incorporate the percent symbol in QuickBooks in order to determine a discount that is equal to one percent of the total. If you don't include this symbol for percentage, QuickBooks supposes you're looking to get the dollar discount, and not an amount discount.

Utilizing the weekly timesheet

For the weekly timesheet option, click the CustomerEnter TimeUse Weekly timesheet command. QuickBooks shows its Weekly Timesheet window. To access this Weekly Timesheet window, first select the Name field in order to determine the name of the worker, the vendor, or any other person who is performing the task. It should be possible to select the person's name in the box labeled Name. If you're unable to choose a name of a person in the Name box add the name of the person in the box. Then when you're asked, tell QuickBooks the name (employee or vendor or any other name) is required to be added. Once you've entered your name as the individual who is performing the work, you can make use of the columns in the Weekly Timesheet window to provide the name of the job or customer for which the work was completed including the service code and a short description or note as well as the pay items (if the

QuickBooks system is used to manage payroll) and the course (if you're keeping track of classes) and finally, the total number of hours each day. You can add as many lines in the weekly timesheet window as you'd like. Each line is displayed separately on the invoice. Notes information appears in the description section in the bottom of your invoice. Therefore, you should use the relevant and informative notes.

Single activity timing

If you would like to record the service activity as it occurs you can select the CustomersEnter TimeTime/Enter Single-Activity command. QuickBooks shows an Time/Enter single activity window.

To record or time an activity in one go, enter the date of the event in the date box. Utilize the name box for identification of the individual responsible for the service. In the Customer:Job box name the person who is performing the service or the task that the service is executed. Choose the appropriate product from the Service Item drop-down list and the correct Payroll items from the Payroll Items drop-down list. When you're tracking class attendance in general, you should make use of the drop-down menu for classes to classify the task. The Notes box is used to write a short but proper review of service. The description is included on your invoice. Therefore, you should be careful about the words you write. After providing or describing this information regarding the service, there are two options for recording the amount of time you spent on the service.

Note down time manually It is possible to record manually the duration of an activity utilising the duration box to record the duration. If you've spent 10 minutes, for instance you can enter 0:10 in the box for Duration. If you've spent three hours and forty minutes then enter 3:40 in the box for Duration.

* Make sure QuickBooks keep track of time It is also possible to use QuickBooks record the amount of time you worked on the task. Click the Start button within the Duration box as you begin your activity and then click the Stop button after you end the activity. If you wish to stop your timer (while you make an important phone call, as an instance) press"Pause.

When you've explained the activity you're doing in the window for Time/Enter Single

Activity Click the Save and New or Save and Close option to store the details of the activity.

Check that the checkbox that says Billable is checked. The checkbox for Billable appears in the upper right part of the Single Activity window. When you select the Billable option you inform QuickBooks that it is required to keep this track of a billable event for later inclusion in an invoice.

You can utilize the buttons Previous and Next which appear on in the upper right-hand corner of the window for Time/Enter Single Activity to navigate back and forth between your activity records. Be aware it is important to note that there is a Spelling button can also be present in the Time/Enter Single Activity window. It is possible to use to click the Spelling button to spell-check the notes description you type in -this is a good option since this information will be later displayed on the invoice.

QuickBooks can also allow your employees to input their hours directly.

Select CustomerEnterTimeLet employees enter their time for details on the way this Web service operates.

Incorporating billable time into an invoice. To add the billable time and expense on an invoice you must create an invoice in the normal method, which I've described earlier. After you have identified the client (and when you've entered the hours for your customer) and, If you've been tracking costs or time for the client, QuickBooks will ask if you'd like to bill for any portion of the costs or time by through a message box. If you answer "yes," QuickBooks displays the Choose Billable Time and Costs dialog box. The Time tab in the Choose Billable Time and Costs dialog box displays each of the times you've recorded for a client. To add these dates to the invoice, simply click the Use column to add the date. If you'd like to choose all dates, click on the Choose All button. After that, click"OK. QuickBooks then adds each of these times to billable lines on the invoice. Click on to open the items, expenses or Mileage tabs to view the lists of the items, expenses out of pocket, or business mileage that are incurred by customers. Charges are added to invoices for these kinds of expenses exactly the same way you do for fees for your time.

Printing Invoices

Print invoices and then mail them in several different ways:

You can print your own invoices by pressing the Print button located at near the bottom on the Create Invoices window.

* You can print invoices in batches by pressing the arrow adjacent to the Print icon, then selecting the Print Batch in the drop-down menu QuickBooks displays in the Select Invoices for Printer dialogue box (which QuickBooks displays) to choose invoices To Be Printed Invoices for printing. Once you have selected the

invoices you wish to print by pressing on them, click OK.

This menu QuickBooks shows when you press the Print arrow has the Preview option. The Preview option to see an example of the invoice that has been printed.

Conclusion

QuickBooks accounting program was created by its developers in such as to be easy to use and extremely user-friendly. After the installation is completed and user setup, the new function provides users with an online orientation exercise. This practice, when combined with this guide will ensure that you get the most of the QuickBooks accounting software and consequently your business. Knowing the way QuickBooks functions is essential for any person who wants to grow their business.

The key to making the success of your small business is effectively managing your customers and, consequently, gaining their loyalty in the event that they refer potential clients to you. Quickbooks makes it easy to enjoy this with an all-encompassing access to the accounts of your customers on one place. You can send out messages, custom reports, and even notifications to your clients. This allows you to increase the value of your products and establish long-term relationships with your clients as well as the marketplace.

www.ingramcontent.com/pod-product-compliance
Lightning Source LLC
Chambersburg PA
CBHW071221210326
41597CB00016B/1904